PURPOSE DRIVEN CAPITAL

Purpose Driven Capital

How to Align Your Money with Your Mission and Multiply Your Impact

Matt Johns

Published by Game Changer Publishing

Paperback ISBN: 978-1-969372-72-8

Hardcover ISBN: 978-1-969372-74-2

Digital ISBN: 978-1-969372-73-5

DISCLAIMER

The information contained in this book is provided solely for educational and informational purposes. It does not constitute, and should not be relied on as, financial, investment, legal, accounting, or tax advice. Readers should consult with their own qualified financial, investment, legal, accounting, and tax professional advisors for personalized advice and conduct their own independent research and due diligence before making any decisions regarding saving, spending, investing, or charitable giving.

Investing always involves risk and the possibility of financial loss. Neither the author nor the publisher makes any guarantee as to investment outcomes or other results from using any information contained in this book, which readers do at their own risk. The author and the publisher disclaim any liability for losses related to readers' use of any information contained in this book.

Purpose Driven Capital and its activities, including any workshops or programs or related materials produced by *Purpose Driven Capital*, constitute outside business activity (OBA) and are completely independent from the author's role as a registered representative and investment adviser representative of any broker-dealer or investment advisory firm with which the author may be associated. No broker-dealer, investment advisory firm, or U.S. federal or state or non-U.S. securities regulatory authority has supervised, reviewed, approved, or endorsed the information contained in this book. This book does not recommend any specific securities, investments, or investing strategies. Any examples provided in this book are hypothetical and are intended solely to illustrate concepts. Past performance is not a guarantee of future results.

www.GameChangerPublishing.com

To Mallory, my beautiful bride, who has lovingly encouraged fifteen years of dreams and wild ideas with endless grace, gently guiding me toward who I'm meant to be.

To Lucy, my wonderful daughter, whose effortless love for life and everyone in it has filled me with awe from her first breath and continues to inspire me more with each passing day.

To Blaise, my incredible son, whose quick wit, desire to learn, and boundless encouragement keep me sharp and my eyes fixed on what's possible and what's right.

AMDG

ADVANCE PRAISE

"Matt's book is great! He not only explains why we need to be more purposeful in ensuring that our investing aligns with our values, but he also provides a logical framework for execution. I recommend this book to anyone who is committed to their values—it's ideal for both individuals and institutions."

— Rich Todd, Principal & CEO, Innovest Portfolio Solutions

"In this book, Matt strikes at the heart of one of the greatest, most overlooked opportunities: getting people to align their allocation of money with their deeply held beliefs. If the 'silent majority' of good people with deeply held and timeless values put their money where their soul is, we'd see the triumph of good over evil on so many fronts. We can no longer separate our profit from our purpose."

— Peter Rex, Founder & CEO, Rex

"Matt has always practiced what he preached, and his newest effort, 'Purpose Driven Capital,' captures his strategies and the impact of those strategies in a thoughtful and practical way. Easy to implement and a lot to think about in these turbulent times. It is well worth the read for anyone who wants their money to go further and do good."

— Susan Winer, Principal and Co-Founder, Strategic Philanthropy Ltd

"'Purpose Driven Capital' by Matt Johns is a masterclass in aligning money with meaning. This book doesn't just inspire; it equips. Johns offers a clear framework that turns financial choices into mission-driven impact. His 'Purpose Switch' is brilliant, showing how values-based decisions unlock clarity and fulfillment. The exclusions and elevations tools are practical game-changers, and the story of Tom Monaghan shows how wealth, redirected toward mission, can transform lives and build legacy.

What sets this book apart is its relentless focus on human dignity. Johns challenges us not only to avoid harm but to elevate our choices to serve the most vulnerable. The Tim Tebow Foundation's work with the 'MVPs' makes this vision come alive. Whether you steward billions or just a hundred dollars, Johns hands you the tools to align resources with mission. 'Purpose Driven Capital' isn't just a book; it's a call to action and a blueprint for turning capital into a force for good."

— Andreas Widmer, Serial Entrepreneur and Founding Director, Ciocca Center for Principled Entrepreneurship at the Catholic University of America

"'Purpose Driven Capital' is an indispensable guide for anyone seeking to align their financial decisions with their deepest values and create a lasting, meaningful impact on the world. Matt Johns provides a practical framework that empowers individuals and organizations to transform their spending, investing, and giving into a powerful force for good, ensuring every dollar contributes to a virtuous legacy."

— Chris Calvert, Vice President of Business Development, J.M. Arbour Wealth Management and Founder, CCAST Holdings

READ THIS FIRST

This book is a tool for you to use the capital in your control to achieve
your purpose—the *why* that gives meaning to every financial decision.
I want to support you on your journey well beyond your reading of this
book. At any time, please visit the link below to download PDF
supplements, access new-content, and engage with others
who are on similar journeys.
Join the movement.

Scan the QR Code Here:

PURPOSE DRIVEN CAPITAL

HOW TO ALIGN YOUR **MONEY** WITH YOUR **MISSION** AND MULTIPLY YOUR **IMPACT**

MATT JOHNS

CONTENTS

INTRODUCTION

ALTRUISTIC FROM BIRTH

I n a quiet room at the Max Planck Institute, a researcher stood before an eighteen-month-old toddler. The child watched curiously as the adult struggled. He had just dropped a clothespin and was reaching out his arms in a lackluster attempt to reach it.

Without saying a word, without being prompted, without receiving any smile, praise, or reward, the child shuffled to the clothespin and picked it up. Then the child looked up at the man and handed him the clothespin.

This happened again and again. In fact, 92 percent of the children under the age of eighteen months did the same thing. Without any motivating factors, no treats, no words of encouragement, they reached out to help.

Psychologists Felix Warneken and Michael Tomasello weren't expecting such a strong result. Their 2006 experiment had a simple goal: They wanted to find out whether human beings are naturally inclined to help others or if people are naturally taught to be generous—the classic nature vs. nurture argument.

To eliminate any social conditioning, they tested toddlers who were too young to understand common manners or earn praise. The children were never told what to do. They were never rewarded. Yet still, time after time, they stepped in to help the struggling adult... an adult with whom they had no prior relationship. By contrast, the chimpanzees in the control group rarely helped and were inconsistent in doing so.

Warneken and Tomasello came to a significant conclusion: The desire to help others, to be generous, is hardwired into each of us. We were created to be altruistic.

You're probably thinking, *Of course! Everybody knows that!* But if that is the case, why do we allow less virtuous actions to persist throughout the world? Why do we continue to do things ourselves that we perceive to be less virtuous?

The reality is that altruism seems to dissipate in life. We may argue that as we mature, we start to understand the ways of the world and realize that things just aren't that simple. But is this true? Perhaps. Or maybe it's just harder to pursue virtue as decisions become more complex.

While altruism may dissipate, it doesn't seem to go away entirely. Almost universally, people have moral limits that define what they will not do. And generally, people have a moral compass directing them to what they believe is right. We may take this as evidence that each of us, to some degree, is at least seeking not to cause harm. But at its core, there is a desire to leave a lasting impact on those around us.

DESIRE FOR IMPACT

There are few areas where we understand the objective value of our contribution to the world better than our finances. While we typically think of this in terms of philanthropy, there is an increasing awareness that all of our financial habits contribute to the good of the world around us.

In 2025, Wells Fargo conducted their annual survey of thousands of investors across the United States. The results revealed a startling fact: 94 percent of American respondents said that they want to make financial decisions that align with their values, a surprising increase from the already high 90 percent they found in their 2024 survey.[1] According to this, nearly every American wishes to use their financial resources for positive purposes.

While our intentions are noble, the reality is that we often make choices that are not in line with our core beliefs. Every day, we unknowingly support causes we oppose. For instance, we may purchase products made in sweatshops or invest in the S&P 500, which likely includes companies engaged in practices we find objectionable. We might also contribute to charities whose programs negatively impact the very communities they aim to help.

Given that many of us are busy taking care of our families and prioritizing immediate needs, we often overlook the broader implications of our financial choices. The complexity of life takes over, so we relax our standards. We may even compromise the altruism we were born with!

ESG: THE PUSH FOR GOOD INTENTIONS

Over the years, several movements have arisen that encourage the use of finances for the greater good:

- **Corporate Social Responsibility** started in the 1950s. It introduced the idea that corporations have responsibilities beyond profit.
- **Socially Responsible Investing** started in the 1960s. It focused on negative screens to avoid harmful industries.
- **Triple Bottom Line** started in the early 1990s. It stated that businesses needed to focus on three measures of success: profit, people, and planet.
- **The United Nations Global Compact** launched in 2000. This movement promoted ten principles in the areas of human rights, labor, the environment, and anti-corruption.

These movements had positive intentions, and some are still around, though they may currently exist in different forms. Regardless of their overall impact, they all contributed to the current most prominent form of social responsibility: ESG.

ESG, which stands for Environmental, Social, and Governance, was introduced by the United Nations in 2004. Since then, it has become the global standard for doing good with financial resources. In fact, it has become so prominent that in 2022, it was the standard for 80 percent of institutional investors.

The ESG movement focuses on its three key areas:

- **Environmental:** How organizations manage their impact on the natural world.
- **Social:** How they affect people, from employees to communities.
- **Governance:** How they are led, including accountability, transparency, and ethical oversight.

It encourages organizations and companies to operate effectively while upholding moral standards. In theory, ESG offers a clear and consistent framework with great promise.

On the positive side, it helps organizations measure and communicate their impact more transparently. Still, the obstacles to implementation remain significant.

Consistent application and a universal definition are required, but these definitions may not align with an individual's personal values.

ESG has become so prominent that it has been codified into a standard, one that, through 2024, public companies and many private companies are widely held up to. In fact, the movement is so prominent and the standards so firm that companies are actually penalized if they do not uphold them. Large institutional investors (banks and large investment funds with significant ownership stakes in these companies) can, and oftentimes do, compel them to conform to ESG standards, threatening to remove their investment if they do not. These pressures can show up in very specific and challenging ways. For example:

- If you are not directly and intentionally pursuing a net-zero carbon policy as they want it to be done, that may lower your "E" score for not having a plan to reduce emissions.

- If your DEI policy (diversity, equity, and inclusion) does not meet their standards or if you don't have one, that will lower your "S" score for not systematically creating opportunities for specific groups of people.
- If your company continues political lobbying or advocacy in areas they disagree with, that can lower your "G" score for not having what they deem acceptable governance.

For individuals and organizations with deeply held convictions, this pressure can lead to very challenging decisions. And therein lies the key problem. This top-down approach ignores two very important aspects of human dignity:

1. The unique gifts of the individual/organization.
2. Agency to pursue virtue through those unique avenues.

I hope we can all agree that some people are more naturally gifted to become NBA basketball players than others. This also applies to less tangible individual gifts and organizational competencies. Some organizations are better built to be activist entities than others. Some are better suited to creating positive change in the environment. However, if the organization is forced to pursue these endeavors and conform to these specific standards, it prevents the full expression of their core competencies and makes it impossible for them to pursue the unique virtues that they *can* offer the world.

This inherently leads to another negative outcome: People will do what it takes to meet the standard, even at the expense of the intended purpose. This is the classic problem of "teaching to the test," where teachers only teach material that will help their students perform well on a standardized test. In the case of ESG, this is often referred to as "greenwashing." This is when organizations misuse ESG metrics solely to achieve the ESG designation, making them more appealing or even merely acceptable to investors or the public. Some entities manipulate the system to enhance their image and gain access to additional resources.

A person may agree with 70 percent of the ESG principles, but the remaining 30 percent can lead to discomfort, as their money would still support those areas with which they disagree. Currently, there is no 70 percent option. Instead, the choice is expressed as "You're either with us or you're against us."

However, there is a BIG silver lining to the ESG movement. It has become a prominent part of the political conversation. Now, corporations and institutional investors aren't the only ones asking about the impact their money is having. Individuals are starting to ask pivotal questions about their investments and contributions: "What causes am I supporting with my money?"

A FRAMEWORK FOR PURPOSE AND VIRTUE WITH YOUR MONEY

This book was written for everyone interested in fulfilling their life's purpose. This is not just for professional investors, philanthropists, the wealthy, or the financially savvy. Every one of us makes decisions about how we spend, invest, and give, and each of those decisions is an opportunity to live with greater purpose and virtue.

Whether you're deciding how to use $100 or $100 million, this framework is for you. Even if you are not ready to develop your own framework, I hope the concepts presented here will help you think more critically about your spending, investing, and giving, and how you can use them to make the impact you want to see in the world.

Unlike most of my colleagues in investment banking, I don't have a decades-long career on Wall Street or in financial services. In fact, I started on what some may consider the opposite path. I began my career working with the poor, then in ministry, then in nonprofits, before entering the world of finance and capital markets. That unorthodox path shaped how I see the role of money in our lives in a unique way. It also shaped how I view money as a tool to be used with intention to drive purpose.

A DIFFERENT PATH

Most people pursue careers and wealth before eventually turning to service. I understood that mine was a different path, but I didn't understand the implications of taking it. All I knew was that I had been given a lot to that point, and I wanted to share it with as many people as I could.

My first professional experience out of college was in the Jesuit Volunteer Corps. That brought me face-to-face with poverty... real, material poverty. I still remember the two Phils who helped me when I first arrived.

As the newly appointed breakfast manager, I had no idea how to take care of the soup kitchen, so the soft-spoken, roll-up-your-sleeves Phil #1 came early from the shelter to help me train volunteers to do it. When he discovered that I didn't know how to cook either, he invited his buddy, the gregarious, outspoken Phil #2 from the shelter to join him.

They came early to help me cook and clean, and I got to know them and their stories. Phil #1 had a medical issue that, over time, left him with no choice but to turn to the streets. Phil #2? Well, I'll just say that the streets were a natural consequence of his choices and actions.

I learned a lot about choices, risk, and misfortune. On the one hand, I saw the value of a dollar to a person in need, how that can not only feed them physically but also bring them hope by feeding their spirit. On the other hand, I learned in a very real way that the same dollar can enable someone to act in a way that further destroys his life and the lives of others. The experience helped me see that the dollar is a tool, and I gained a deeply visceral understanding of how it can impact people.

From there, I moved into youth ministry, where questions were less about day-to-day survival and more about why we exist. This is where I was forced to dig into the "why" of this world... our purpose.

If you've spent any time around teenagers, you know the kinds of questions they ask and their earnestness in posing them. Where did we come from? Why do bad things happen to good people? How could God create something that is not good? How do we trust people and institutions that do bad things? How are we supposed to treat others who disagree with us? Why do I exist?

Some questions have straightforward answers. Some remain mysteries throughout this life. As I listened to these questions from thousands of teens, I became keenly aware of the human perspective.

Frankly, we all have these questions, but as adults, we often lack the humility to ask them out loud, or we simply don't have the mental bandwidth to give them the attention we would like. Because it was my job, I was not only able to face these questions; I was enabled to take the time and mental bandwidth to address them, find answers, and ask next-level questions that would shape my perspective for life.

Then I made an interesting transition to a large nonprofit. This is where I started to see the direct effect of money on people's lives. I had the chance to work with prominent community leaders, people whose decisions had real effects on others. I spent time with some of the most affluent in our community, people who had built incredible businesses and sought to do tremendous good. I also spent considerable time with those who had nothing to their name... arguably less than nothing when taking into account their debts. Our nonprofit served as the bridge between these two worlds, and I held an incredible role that allowed me to see all sides of it.

My experience during Hurricane Harvey offers a distinct snapshot of this period in my life. I was highly integrated into regional disaster recovery at the time. I had been unwittingly voted into a position of leadership among the nonprofits and government organizations that responded to disasters. Notably, natural disasters are not uncommon in the Greater Houston area. We had just responded to three federally declared flooding events in the last two years, so another flood was highly likely.

At the time, Hurricane Harvey was the second costliest disaster in U.S. history. Tens of thousands of Southeast Texas families were left without homes or possessions. Many were financially able to rebuild on their own, but many others were not. Because of my position, I had been in the regional emergency operations center, helping coordinate efforts with all of the top officials during the storm. I was in constant communication with organizational and government leaders, ensuring that survivors' needs were met in the direst of circumstances.

It was an incredible experience. On the one hand, I was engaging national leaders. This included the leaders of large national disaster recovery organizations and the nation's largest nonprofit funders. I even had the honor of being invited to join the mayor and county judge to welcome President Donald Trump for his visit and tour of the main recovery center.

However, I also met survivors, people who had lost everything. During the storm, I helped field emergency calls from people who were standing on their kitchen counters, begging for rescue. I also met people in their homes, where they were still living months after the storm. I will never forget the overwhelming stench of black mold I experienced time and again.

Over the following years, I worked closely with case managers, directing donor funds to these families to help them rebuild their lives. I also helped convey the stories of those who were impacted to donors. This is one of the great superpowers of nonprofits.

For nonprofits, their value is not in money; it is in their mission. They are responsible for generating community support for that mission. As a result, they know how to communicate social outcomes in non-financial terms—a lesson that is deeply rooted in this framework.

I spent considerable time with donors and understood why they chose to give. Their reasons were all deeply similar—to help people— but their purpose was always unique. They each hoped to accomplish something more than simply helping people rebuild their lives.

So, how did I get into investment banking from here?

CAPITAL TO BUILD THE WORLD

I had been pursuing a career as a nonprofit CEO, so I heeded our CEO's recommendation to get an advanced degree. While pursuing my MBA, I realized that I really enjoyed finance, so I decided to explore how I could leverage my experience and passion for my values to pursue a career in that industry.

This eventually led to my starting my own investment bank, Honey-Hive Capital. I understood the power that capital has to influence global actions and outcomes. Investment bankers have a unique role in this process, and I saw an opportunity to move millions or even billions of dollars in a positive direction in the world.

I quickly realized that the private markets were the best place for me to do that. Whereas public markets focus mostly on the valuation of existing businesses, like Apple, Google, and Amazon, private markets build something from nothing. They fund real estate developments and help businesses grow. I like to say that private markets are where the dirt gets tilled to build the world.

As an investment bank, we work with investors who allocate billions of dollars every day. These include large institutional pensions, endowments, banks, and investment advisors, as well as family offices and ultra-high-net-worth families. I am always amazed by the depth of thought and care that the people behind these decisions apply to their work. They genuinely understand the magnitude of their decisions on their organizations, beneficiaries, and even the world writ large. And yes, they treat their roles accordingly.

HoneyHive Capital occupies a unique niche in this space. It has a faith-aligned approach. While we work with people of all faiths or no faith all the time, we ensure that every deal we offer passes through our negative screen to ensure that they do not violate traditional Christian values, my personal values. We also apply a positive screen to highlight deals that uphold the same Christian values. I am excited to share more about how to apply this structure to your values later in this book.

THE GOOD, THE TRUE, AND THE BEAUTIFUL

My firm's goal is to direct capital toward genuine virtue in pursuit of the good, the true, and the beautiful. For millennia, philosophers and theologians have recognized these as what we now refer to as the transcendentals.

The reason they matter is simple. The Transcendentals are what every human being ultimately longs for. The good is the draw to ethical and virtuous actions. The truth refers to understanding and accepting reality as it truly is. The beautiful is, at its essence, order and harmony in the world. These are not abstract ideas reserved for philosophers—they are the deepest desires of the human heart, and they give shape to the purpose to which we all aspire.

Thinkers across history have recognized this. Plato and Aristotle first laid the groundwork, tying human flourishing to ultimate realities like truth and goodness. Augustine carried the insight further, speaking of God as Truth itself and Beauty "ever ancient, ever new." Aquinas then gave the transcendentals their most formal expression, showing how truth, goodness, and beauty flow from the very nature of being itself.

Taken together, these voices remind us that the transcendentals are not a luxury or a curiosity. They are a universal inheritance, the signposts of our deepest pursuit, and the ultimate destination for our work, our lives, and, of course, our capital.

So, what does this mean for the capital you influence? Every financial decision you make is ultimately a choice about the kind of world you want to help create. And in each of those choices, the transcendentals are at play. Does this purchase or investment reflect what is truly good? Does it align with what is real and true about how the world works? Does it contribute something beautiful that uplifts humanity?

The problem is that most of us make these choices unconsciously. We spend on convenience without considering if it's truly good. We invest in whatever promises returns without asking if it's in pursuit of truth. We support causes that make us feel good, but we don't ensure they actually lead to positive outcomes.

The Purpose-Driven Capital Framework helps you make these choices intentionally, aligning your deepest values with your daily financial decisions.

I hope that this book will help you in your pursuit of the good, the true, and the beautiful. Each of us is endowed with unique gifts and abilities. As such, each of us is called to do something unique in our brief time in this world. We often think about legacy, but how many of us have a clear plan to create one?

FIND YOUR SOLUTION

The book has three parts:

1. Know your purpose.
2. Guide your desired outcomes.
3. Build your process.

Part I covers how to clearly define your true purpose and craft a Purpose Statement—the foundational *why* that explains your existence. You can then translate that purpose into a mission, the *what* and *how* that give it form. Together, purpose and mission become the basis for the framework and for your personal or organizational existence.

In Part II, we will look at how to ensure that your actions lead you to your desired outcomes. These outcomes are not simply what you want to accomplish, but your legacy.

Then, in Part III, we will take actionable steps to build your process. We will build on the mindset and framework, helping you see how to turn abstract decisions into an objective process.

THE PURPOSE-DRIVEN CAPITAL FRAMEWORK: YOUR FLIGHT PLAN

You can use this book in two ways. First, you can take it as a framework for your perspective and incorporate it into your financial decision-making process. Or, it can be a complete system to align your financial decisions with your mission. You can think of it as a flight plan that begins with your Purpose Statement and charts a mission-aligned course toward your desired impact on the world.

Here is a high-level overview of what you can expect from the following chapters.

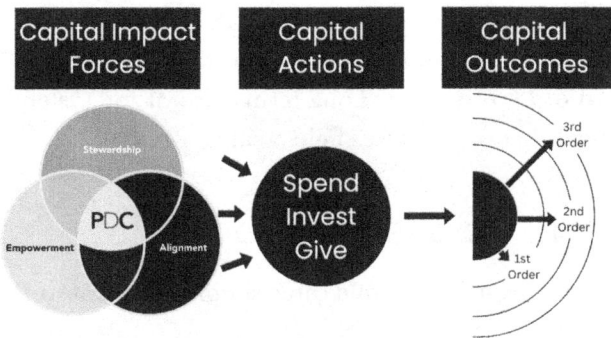

THE FOUNDATION: THE THREE CAPITAL IMPACT FORCES

Like an airplane needs thrust, steering, and stability to reach its destination, your financial decisions need three coordinated forces:

- **Stewardship:** How you manage and grow your resources responsibly
- **Empowerment:** How your money serves and uplifts people
- **Alignment:** How your choices stay consistent with your deepest values

THE ACTIONS: WHERE YOUR MONEY GOES

Every dollar you control flows through one of three channels:

- **Spending:** Trading money for goods and services you need
- **Investing:** Putting money to work to grow while supporting businesses and ideas
- **Giving:** Directing resources toward causes without expecting financial return

THE OUTCOMES: YOUR IMPACT ON THE WORLD

Your financial choices create ripple effects that extend far beyond the immediate transaction:

- **First-order outcomes:** Direct, immediate results
- **Second-order outcomes:** Follow-on effects that impact others
- **Third-order outcomes:** Long-term cultural and systemic changes that your choices help create

YOUR THREE ASSESSMENT TOOLS

To make this practical, you'll build three simple tools that work together:

1. **Purpose Assessment:** Does this align with my purpose and values?
2. **Exclusions Screen:** Does this violate any of my morals or ethics?
3. **Elevations Assessment:** Does this advance my most important goals?

Once you build your system with your purpose in mind, you can intentionally and consistently direct your actions toward the outcomes you want to see in the world.

I want to empower you to make your unique impact, measure it, and share it with the world in a way that brings others into your mission.

So, whether your mission is 100 percent in line with ESG standards or not—or whatever the standard happens to be today—you can create a system that allows your purpose to define and express your desired impact.

I believe that we are all driven to pursue virtue, genuine virtue. I also believe that everyone is seeking the good, the true, and the beautiful. However, we all seek them in our own unique ways. Each of us has been given unique gifts, passions, and perspectives to offer the world. And those gifts should be free to flourish, not confined to a narrow checklist of what others say is good or valuable. When your capital is aligned with your purpose and your unique gifts, it becomes a force for impact that no one else can replicate.

A WARNING

If you enjoy moving through life without considering the impact of your financial decisions on the rest of the world, this book is likely going to disrupt that. It will help you confront a lot of the difficult realities that are both in front of us and worlds away.

However, if you want to go deeper and use your capital to live a life of significance, this book will help you do so.

The Purpose-Driven Capital Framework is your starting point. I believe that I have been given a tremendous gift in taking this different path. From the feedback I have received, this perspective seems to resonate with many. I hope it resonates with you, too, in a way that allows you and your organization to use your capital to build the world you envision and leave a lasting legacy.

PART ONE
KNOW YOUR PURPOSE

CHAPTER 1
FUND YOUR PURPOSE, DEFEAT YOUR ADVERSARY

If our goal is to direct our capital toward genuine virtue in the pursuit of the good, the true, and the beautiful, we must commit our resources to our purpose and defeat what opposes it.

FINANCING THE MOONSHOT

t was a moment that changed the trajectory of all humankind, an event unlike anything else in human history. Six hundred million people around the world were focused on their TVs, watching the grainy image of a man climbing down the stairs of the now-famous spider-like structure onto a foreign celestial body. Humans had innovated a path to land one of their own on the moon.

People had been on Earth for two hundred thousand years before Orville and Wilbur Wright accomplished the impossible with their fifty-nine-second flight at Kitty Hawk, North Carolina. Just sixty-six years later, three people traveled 240,000 miles, and two of them landed on the distant body of our night sky.

Neil Armstrong was just the tip of an enormous spear. To accomplish this goal with less computing power than a handheld calculator, more than four hundred thousand people were engaged in one aspect or another to support the Apollo Program.

His words remain immortal: "That's one small step for man; one giant leap for mankind." Armstrong was so focused on the mission at hand that he did not even finalize his first words until shortly before landing. Amazingly, no one, not even mission control, knew what he was going to say.

These words perfectly express what was accomplished. His literal steps off the man-made moon lander onto the moon's surface were the culmination of an incredible technological, political, and even philosophical milestone. It was a triumph of human collaboration, vision, and will.

While it is often challenging to imagine the technical and engineering feats that were involved in making this possible, it is almost inconceivable to consider the political achievement of getting an entire nation to back this seemingly impossible goal.

This accomplishment for "all mankind" cost the American taxpayers $25.8 billion, or $300 billion in 2025 dollars. The American public was in a tremendous period of unrest. The Cold War had gripped the country, and the Soviet Union was not afraid to flex its muscles. Their launch of Sputnik in 1957 created an entirely new fear for the American people. Oceans and airspace were no longer sufficient barriers. The enemy could be floating above our heads at any given moment.

When John F. Kennedy took office, he was keenly aware of the Soviet threat. He recognized that the U.S. needed to flex its own muscles and act swiftly to gain the upper hand in the Cold War. He knew that space was the ultimate stage for supremacy.

NACA (eventually NASA) was reactively formed in 1958, and by the time Kennedy took office, it only had 8000 employees and a $400 million budget. At this point, the Soviets not only launched the first artificial satellite. They also sent Luna 2 to the Moon. And just three months after Kennedy took office, they launched Yuri Gagarin into orbit.

The U.S. was perceived as inferior by just about all conceivable measures. Kennedy wanted to gain the upper hand, but he knew that he needed public support to make it happen.

Just three weeks after Gagarin's flight, NASA successfully launched Alan Shepard in the Mercury spacecraft Freedom 7. Though the flight was suborbital, an American made it to space.

Just twenty days after Shepard's flight, Kennedy took the podium before Congress. He set the mission that led to the "one small step for man" just eight years later: "I believe that this nation should commit itself to achieving the goal, before this decade is out, of landing a man on the Moon and returning him safely to the Earth."

Considering the technological struggles, this was a bold mission for America. But it worked.

Kennedy then took his plea to the public. In September 1962, he spoke about the nation's space effort at Rice University. He directed this to the American people, and it was memorable. "We choose to go to the Moon in this decade and do the other things, not because they are easy, but because they are hard."[1]

And so it began.

President Kennedy set the nation on a path toward Purpose-Driven Capital. He set forth a clear mission, and he identified the purpose behind the difficulty that it would create. As a result, the taxpayers of the United States directed 4 percent of the federal budget toward this ambitious goal, leading to one of the greatest achievements in human history.

MISSION FOR THE GREATER GOOD

JFK painted a vision that shaped world history. He did this at a bleak time. The Soviets had won every component of the space race. The U.S. had only achieved suborbital flight. Nobody knew how reaching the Moon was possible, but Kennedy painted a vision that made the impossible seem possible. It was a destination that would allow battles to be lost because it would ultimately win the war.

This mission gave the American people a shared sense of direction. Congress approved funding for the project. The American people, while not entirely united, backed it enough to continue to elect representatives to office who would continue the funding. The concept of "what could be" was in the nation's psyche. The moonshot succeeded because the nation's mission served a clear purpose: freedom's triumph over fear.

This is what happens when we create frameworks in our lives. We start to see things differently. We start to avoid things that are not in line with that framework and pursue things that further our purpose. When our minds are focused, we accomplish great things.

This is obviously true with our finances. Our money dictates what we do with our lives. For example, when we are focused on buying our first home, we make decisions in line with that purchase. To save for a down payment, we avoid buying unnecessary things. We start thinking about the best locations for long-term value appreciation and the schools where our kids will be educated. When we consider borrowing money, we think about how that will impact our ability to obtain a mortgage.

When going through this process, we think long-term. We are on a mission to serve our purpose. We think about how our decisions today will affect us and those closest to us tomorrow.

WIRED FOR PURPOSE: THE PURPOSE SWITCH

As stated in the introduction, the vast majority of people want to make financial decisions in line with their values, but it is clear that most people do not live up to that aspiration. The difference isn't intelligence, wealth, or opportunity. The difference is understanding how your brain works.

Let me give you an example. Consider two scenarios. You discover your 401(k) supports companies that profit from gambling addiction, seeming to contradict your commitment to protect vulnerable people. Far too often, people may feel uncomfortable but ultimately decide "everyone invests in diversified funds." However, some may immediately begin researching investment options that exclude predatory industries. What separates these two responses? The second person is responding to their Purpose Switch.

There is a switch in your brain that I call the "Purpose Switch." When this switch is off, life continues. You work. You build. You achieve things. But something feels fundamentally wrong. Something is missing. You can't put your finger on it, but you know it's there.

Your brain never stops asking one question: Does this matter? We think this voice comes from our heart, but it's actually biological. It's hard-wired into how we're built.

The Purpose Switch operates through systems designed to connect what we believe with what we do. When you make financial decisions that align with your stated values, your prefrontal cortex—your brain's command center—recognizes the harmony between belief and action. This recognition activates your reward pathways, creating satisfaction that comes not from what you get, but from who you become through the choice.

Deep in your brain, there exists a network that links meaning, motivation, and action. Scientists call it the reward system. Dopamine pathways illuminate when you're moving in the right direction, when your actions serve your purpose.

But here's what happens when you betray your own values with your money: Your brain detects the contradiction. Specialized regions sound an alarm. You experience cognitive dissonance—that persistent feeling that something is "off" even when you can't explain why.

When your choices align with your purpose and your actions express your beliefs, the Purpose Switch activates. Your brain stops fighting itself. Clarity emerges because your internal systems work in harmony rather than conflict. You feel motivated because your reward center fully engages. You feel fulfilled because everything inside you points in the same direction.

The Purpose Switch creates its own momentum. Each values-aligned decision makes the next one easier. Each aligned choice strengthens the pathways between moral reasoning and reward.

Over time, purposeful decisions feel natural, while contradictory choices become uncomfortable.

The Purpose Switch becomes self-reinforcing. Once activated, your reward system craves more alignment. It deepens your connection to purpose and creates a positive cycle that pulls you toward better choices.

This is how we're designed. Purpose isn't a luxury—it's a biological necessity. The way you use money either activates this system or fights against it. And that choice shapes everything that follows.

DEFINING CAPITAL: HISTORY AND PHILOSOPHY

What is capital? At its core, capital is an inherently social model that enhances one's ability to generate value. It can be used to create value across various categories, including financial, social, physical, and intellectual. In his seminal work, *Family Wealth*, James Hughes identifies three primary sources of capital: financial, human, and intellectual. While all of these play an important role in daily life for families, individuals, and organizations, this book will primarily focus on financial capital.

This brings us to the question: How did money, as we know it today, emerge as a source of capital? Money hasn't always existed. Historically, value was exchanged through a barter system, where individuals traded goods and services directly. For instance, a farmer might trade wheat for a blacksmith's tools.

However, this system presented a challenge known as the "double coincidence of wants." This means that for a trade to occur, both parties must possess what the other requires. For example, if the blacksmith doesn't want wheat, there's no mutual agreement, and the trade cannot happen. An intermediary source, a universally accepted store of value, is necessary to overcome this problem.

For a common medium to be effective as a widely used store of value, it must possess five key characteristics:

1. **Widely Accepted:** It must be trusted and accepted by a broad group of people.
2. **Divisible:** It should be easily divisible so that it can accommodate small and large transactions (e.g., a hundred-pound chunk of gold must be able to be divided to purchase a loaf of bread).
3. **Durable:** The medium must be able to withstand the test of time and preserve its value.
4. **Portable:** It should be easy to transport, allowing it to move from person to person and place to place.
5. **Hard to Counterfeit:** It must be difficult to replicate without something backing it as a true source of value.

Now, let's take a look at the evolution of money.

Over time, money has progressed, reflecting a growing balance between efficiency and trust. In the beginning, people engaged in barter, trading items of intrinsic value, such as shells, salt, beads, or even cattle. These items were easily tradable within communities because, if everyone needed beads, for example, they could easily exchange them for necessities like bread. The intrinsic value of beads made them a suitable medium of exchange within that community.

However, problems arose when attempting to trade outside of that community, as beads might not hold the same value elsewhere. This is when societies started to adopt more universally accepted items, like precious metals. Metals had common value and could be distributed in clearly defined denominations, originally based on weight.

Eventually, precious metals evolved into coinage. These coins were backed not only by their weight in precious metal but also by the authority of the issuing government. As coins became cumbersome to carry, the need arose for a way to represent these values without the physical weight. This led to the creation of paper money, which represented stores of coins.

Over time, money became more intertwined with financial institutions. The trust we placed in these institutions allowed paper money to evolve further, eventually leading us to a system where we don't even use physical currency. Today, we often rely on numbers on a screen to represent value in financial transactions.

There are three key functions of money:

1. **Medium of Exchange:** We use money to buy goods and services.
2. **Unit of Account:** Money provides a way to measure value, such as stating a price in dollars.
3. **Store of Value:** Money retains its value over time, allowing us to hold on to it without needing to exchange it immediately.

Money is a social construct based on trust among individuals. This trust can lead to various social outcomes, which we should examine closely.

CAPITAL CONFUSION

Money has become an integral part of our lives. Human nature has driven its creation. That begs the question: What happens when we are not directing our capital toward our purpose?

This can happen to us easily. I remember watching a local news story that went viral. The local county government had just passed an ordinance requiring all of its vehicles to be electric. The reporter was at the charging stations attached to a government building, interviewing a county official, who was proudly showing off the fleet they had just purchased as they charged.

When the reporter calmly asked the official if she knew what the power source was for the charging stations, she bluntly said that it was the same as the building. The reporter then asked if the building was using power derived from the local coal power plant. The immediate pause and look away was a physical representation of her capital confusion.

It isn't hard to relate to when our actions are out of alignment with our mission or purpose. While the county official had great intentions to pursue the common good, she clearly had not thought through all of the factors involved in achieving her intended outcome. Her face showed her discomfort as she was clearly trying to move away from coal-fueled pollution. Friction, stress, noise, and doubt all alert us to something being "off."

Many people and institutions have strong values and make financial decisions with good intentions, yet these actions are often taken without a clear purpose. People tend to spend reactively, invest passively, and give inconsistently, primarily because their purpose and subsequent mission remain unclear.

They lack a unified strategy and often fail to recognize that they are combining various issues. This confusion eventually leads to poor results. Their decisions may become clearer, but their intentions conflict, creating a sense of chaos and loss of control.

As a consequence, the focus shifts to the action itself rather than the intent or the outcome, which can result in negative consequences. These outcomes may violate their ethical standards and fund broken systems.

Most tragically, they squander opportunities to create a better world in alignment with their deeply held values. This leads many to question whether they are using their capital in line with their personal beliefs, let alone making a difference with their financial resources. When organizations remain indifferent, confused, and in pain, they invite an opposing force to fill the void—one actively working against their mission.

YOUR ADVERSARY

There's something you need to understand before we go any further. You have an adversary—not in some abstract, philosophical sense, but in the most practical, financial reality of your daily life. Beyond the normal constraints and challenges we all face, there are entities that systematically benefit when you fail to live according to your purpose.

Your Adversary isn't necessarily a specific person plotting against you in a back room somewhere. Instead, they are those who want your mission to fail and their counter-mission to succeed. While you've been busy with life, your Adversary has been busy building systems designed to oppose your mission.

So, who is your Adversary? Your Adversary could be individuals, institutions, or entire industries that profit when you remain confused, passive, or indifferent about your financial choices. They benefit from your "capital confusion," the disconnect between your stated values and your actual financial decisions.

Here's how to identify them. Ask yourself, *Who stands to lose if I accomplish my vision for the world?* If you're passionate about environmental sustainability, your Adversary includes anyone who profits from environmental destruction. If you care about human dignity, your Adversary includes anyone who exploits people for profit. If you want to strengthen families, your Adversary includes anyone whose business model depends on family breakdown.

So, how do you enable their counter-mission? Your Adversary has studied you better than you've studied them. They know exactly how to keep you funding their operations while you think you're being responsible with the capital in your control.

First, they exploit your fear and indecision. When you hesitate to make values-aligned financial choices because they seem complicated or costly, you create a void that defaults to their benefit. Every investment you don't research, every purchase you don't investigate, and every donation you don't evaluate flows through systems they've designed.

Second, they count on your unconscious funding. Right now, your retirement account may include companies that directly oppose your deepest values. Your daily purchases potentially support supply chains that violate your conscience. Your bank deposits may fund loans to industries you'd never knowingly support. You're not doing this intentionally. And that's exactly how they want it!

Third, they depend on your passive indifference. Your Adversary's greatest weapon isn't being your opposition. It's your assumption that your choices don't matter. You think, *What difference can one person or one organization make?* That's exactly what they want you to think.

So, why does this matter? Your Adversary is organized, strategic, and patient. They've spent years building systems that make harmful choices convenient and beneficial choices difficult. They've made it easier for you to fund what you oppose than to support what you believe.

Here's what they didn't count on. Once you see the connection between your money and your purpose, you can't unsee it! Once you understand that every dollar you control has the potential to either advance your values or undermine them, it becomes really hard to look past it.

The Purpose-Driven Capital Framework isn't just about making better financial decisions. It's about recognizing that you're already in a battle for your values. Your Adversary has been playing this game while you didn't even know the game existed. But now you do.

Throughout this book, we'll show you how your Adversary operates and how to defeat them by aligning your capital with your mission.

PURPOSE-DRIVEN CAPITAL: YOUR OFFENSIVE STRATEGY

What if you had a logical solution or system to empower your spending, investing, and giving? This system would drive the outcomes you wish to achieve in the world and actively counter your Adversary.

Imagine if you had full mission clarity and understood your purpose completely. What if you could implement a process that aligns all of your actions with your purpose, guiding you toward your desired outcomes? With the right system in place, you can intentionally and consistently drive the outcomes you want to see in the world.

I want to help you build your unique, mission-aligned system to spend, invest, and give. My goal is to help you make decisions more easily. If you follow this book, you'll create a system consisting of four core tools:

1. **Purpose Statement**
2. **Purpose Alignment Evaluation**
3. **Exclusions Screen**
4. **Elevations Assessment**

In addition to those four tools, you'll learn an actionable step-by-step approach to analyze decisions and determine whether the potential reward is worth the risk.

Purpose-Driven Capital is the strategic allocation of your financial resources through spending, investing, and giving, guided by the principles of Stewardship, Empowerment, and Alignment. This approach consistently produces intentional, values-based outcomes. I developed this system for your benefit because I want to empower you to bring your values to light in the world.

CHAPTER 2
THE PURPOSE-DRIVEN CAPITAL FRAMEWORK

If our goal is to direct our capital toward genuine virtue in the pursuit
of the good, the true, and the beautiful, we need a model that
connects our purpose to real-world impact.
This is the Purpose-Driven Capital Framework.

t has been estimated that people make between 33,000 and 35,000 decisions per day. Most of these are unconscious decisions. That may seem outrageous, but if you think about it, you are actively deciding right now whether to continue reading this paragraph or accomplish some other task. Every action requires a decision.

We would go crazy if we had to critically analyze every single conscious and unconscious decision we make in a day. Consider the thought process we go through when we decide where to take someone for lunch. We often run through an entire cost-benefit analysis that ranges from fast food to Brazilian steakhouse.

This is generally true for all decisions, whether big or small. Structure is what gives us the ability to build. Structure eases analysis paralysis and enables us to be productive. For instance, routines offer a structure that allows us to accomplish mundane tasks while reducing the brainpower required, thanks to habit. Frameworks, models, routines... all help us operate efficiently.

The key to structure is focus. To what end are we directing these actions and decisions? We build our morning routine to efficiently accomplish all the small tasks that sufficiently prepare us for the day, ideally with as little thinking as possible.

When considering major financial decisions, we are greatly served when we know what end we hope to serve in the world and what we want our resources to accomplish. When you know your mission and have a set of criteria in mind, those decisions are not only easier to make, but they will tend to move toward your mission more often than not. That is the goal of the Purpose-Driven Capital Framework.

THE THREE BRICKLAYERS

A traveler came upon a construction site where three bricklayers were working. Curious, he approached the first and asked, "What are you doing?"

With a grunt, the man replied, "I'm laying bricks." His voice sounded tired, his movements were routine, and he focused solely on the wall in front of him.

The traveler then moved on to the second bricklayer and asked the same question. This worker replied, "I'm building a wall." He looked up briefly and smiled faintly, suggesting that he understood he was a part of something slightly larger than just laying bricks.

Finally, the traveler approached the third bricklayer and asked again, "What are you doing?"

The third man stood tall, his eyes bright and full of purpose. Wiping the sweat from his brow, he said with pride, "I'm building a cathedral."

The first bricklayer was merely going through the motions. He was passive and did not see the bigger picture. The second bricklayer grasped that he was part of a larger purpose but didn't have the full picture. The third bricklayer, however, truly understood the grand plan. He recognized that each brick was part of something not just bigger, but magnificent, something that would be seen and used for a greater purpose for many generations to come—maybe even something that represented the deeply held convictions and beliefs that he wanted to help realize.

The third worker had likely seen the architectural drawings and understood what the cathedral would look like. More importantly, he grasped the meaning behind what he was building. He was motivated by a vision aligned with his personal beliefs, knowing that his small action today would lead to a beautiful, lasting outcome for future generations.

This serves as an illustration for all of us because it is easy to become caught up in our daily routines. Without a sense of purpose and order, our actions can feel meaningless, mere tasks to reach a momentary goal, yet every action has consequences.

These outcomes can vary greatly based on our intentions. With the right perspective, we can take deliberate actions and create something meaningful and enduring. We're not just aiming for immediate results; we're also striving for a legacy that lasts for generations.

The Purpose-Driven Capital Framework is designed to help you use your financial resources to achieve something that aligns with your values and vision for the world.

YOUR ADVERSARY WANTS YOU TO BE DISORDERED

Your Adversary understands something crucial about human psychology: Decision fatigue disables the Purpose Switch. When you're overwhelmed by complex choices, comparing hundreds of investment options, analyzing competing ESG ratings, or sorting through contradictory impact claims, the Switch becomes overloaded. The cognitive resources needed to connect decisions with values get depleted.

This is exactly what your Adversary wants. When your Purpose Switch is offline due to decision fatigue, you default to convenient choices rather than conscious ones. You invest in whatever everyone else does, buy from whatever vendor is cheapest, or give to whatever charity sends the most compelling direct mail. Your Adversary profits from your mental exhaustion. Your Adversary thrives on your confusion about the impact your financial decisions actually have. They want you to see your spending, investing, and giving as separate, unrelated activities rather than three parts of one integrated system.

Your Adversary wants you to make financial decisions reactively. They don't want you to understand how each choice connects to your larger purpose. They want you to spend unconsciously, invest passively, and give emotionally—all while missing how these actions can work in concert.

Their strategy is to overwhelm you with options while hiding the connections between your choices and their outcomes. They want you to think that your individual decisions don't matter... that the system is too complex for you to navigate it intentionally.

So, what does your Adversary fear you'll do? That you'll develop a systematic approach to your financial choices. That you'll see how a purpose-aligned approach can amplify your purpose rather than create systems that fight against each other.

When your purpose is clear and your process is systematic, your Adversary loses their greatest weapon, your internal disorder. The Purpose-Driven Capital Framework transforms scattered decisions into focused action.

DEFEATING YOUR ADVERSARY

You need to construct your system with the purpose of intentionally opposing your Adversary in pursuit of your mission.

This leads to the central question: How can I intentionally create the outcomes I want to see in the world in alignment with my values?

The Purpose-Driven Capital Framework will streamline your decision-making process so it aligns with your mission and goals. It will help you know your purpose, build your process, and guide your outcomes.

A strong mission is the result of a clearly defined purpose that serves as the foundation for all decisions made by you, your organization, or your team. Building your process involves creating a decision-making system that becomes second nature to you and your organization.

Lastly, this purpose, which shapes the process, will guide the outcomes you seek. This means your process becomes the driving force behind these outcomes, allowing you to take control of your capital and its impact on the world.

INTRODUCTION TO THE MODEL

Every time you spend, invest, and give, there are outcomes. When it comes to your purpose, these outcomes can either enable your purpose or harm it. I presume that your goal is to enable the positive and avoid the negative.

Positive outcomes could be anything from buying something you need to helping a company you like get off the ground to serving people in the community through a charity you support.

Negative outcomes can be anything from encouraging slave labor to funding corruption to even harming the economy at large.

The biggest problem we face is our ignorance. Typically, we don't see or even consider the outcomes of our spending, investing, and giving. This model will provide a framework to help you get a better picture of how your mindset shapes your financial decisions so that they lead to the outcomes you want to see in the world.

The Purpose-Driven Capital Framework is intentionally simple on its face and should be intuitive to each of us. Individually, we make dozens of financial decisions each day, so this is unquestionably our lived experience.

There are three sections in the image below: Capital Impact Forces, Capital Actions, and Capital Outcomes.

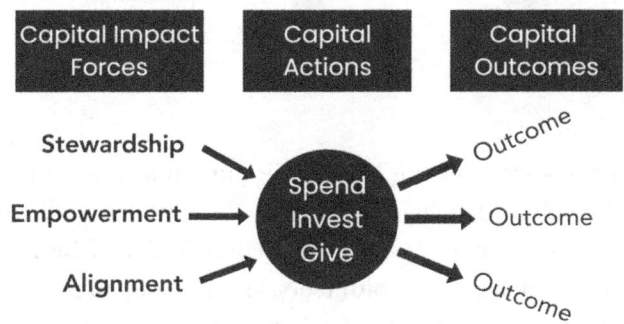

Let's start in the middle with the three Capital Actions: spending, investing, and giving. These are tangible financial decisions that result in Capital Outcomes, indicated by the arrows pointing to the right. These outcomes may range from a simple item purchase to a corporate giant producing more of a widget on a global scale.

However, on the far left are the three Capital Impact Forces: Stewardship, Empowerment, and Alignment. These are the fundamental driving forces that influence our decisions. The Capital Impact Forces are the key to understanding the concept, the linchpin to the entire model.

I've mentioned that nonprofits have a superpower. This is how their mission-focused mindset can be used in our personal or business finances to drive our mission.

This model is based on a common structure for nonprofits, the logic model. Logic models are used to assess nonprofit programs. They provide a visual roadmap that links resources and actions to the results achieved. They are not identical, but both illustrate a very similar thought process.

There are three primary parts to the basic logic model: Inputs, Outputs, and Outcomes.

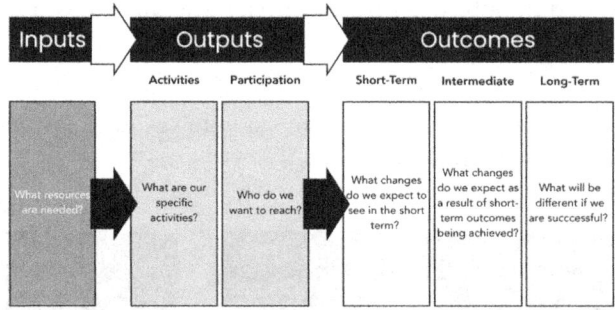

Logic models start on the left with inputs. Inputs are the resources needed to launch and sustain a program, like money, staff, volunteers, time, equipment, partnerships, data, etc. For a food distribution line, this would include staff, location, volunteers, and the food to be distributed.

The inputs then feed the outputs in the middle section. These are the actions or strategies that are carried out through the program—the actual work being accomplished and the participants who benefit from those activities. For food distribution, this is the actual distribution activity and the recipients of the food.

The inputs then lead to outputs. These are the immediate results of the activity. For the food distribution, this is the measurable amount of food distributed to a number of people.

The outputs then lead to outcomes. These are actual results of the program, ideally measurable, beyond the productivity of the activities. In the food distribution example, there is more to the story than families receiving food. That food should have some kind of benefit for them. What does the gift of that food enable them to accomplish? Does it eventually lead them to become self-sufficient? (We'll dive more into this in Chapter 8 when we discuss measurements.)

As I hope you'll see, the Purpose-Driven Capital Framework is very similar. This is where the mission-focused superpower of nonprofits can enable each of us to use our finances to guide our financial decisions. When we apply this holistic mindset to the three Capital Actions, we start thinking in terms of outcomes rather than actions.

However, the key to this is not the outcomes. It is actually the three Capital Impact Forces. To better understand this, let's take a closer look at each vertical section of the Purpose-Driven Capital Framework.

THREE CAPITAL ACTIONS

These are the three fundamental actions that are performed with money: spending, investing, and giving. Capital Actions are based on our belief system. When we are clear about what we believe and want to accomplish, the actions tend to follow. As a result, the outcomes tend to align with those beliefs. However, even well-intentioned actions can result in unfavorable outcomes. This is what your Adversary is counting on!

Therefore, it's important to consider the various Capital Impact Forces that drive actions, leading to the outcomes we desire in the world. Let's take a closer look at each of the three Capital Actions.

Spending: Spending is the action of trading capital, which serves as a store of value, for a good or service, without anticipating anything in return other than that specific item or service. This is the act of buying something, a transaction, and it can be as simple as buying a candy bar or as complex as a government contract to build a lunar lander.

Investing: Investing, on the other hand, is the act of trading capital in exchange for a stake in something, with the expectation of receiving a financial return that exceeds the initial investment. For example, if we invest in a company, we are providing funds in the hope that the company will generate greater value over time, resulting in an increase in our investment. This could be an investment in the stock market or paying for an education.

Giving: Giving refers to providing capital to support others without any expectation of a good, service, or financial gain in return. Instead, we hope and expect that our contributions will be used for some type of social good that benefits others and, in a broader sense, can positively impact society as a whole.

What about saving or borrowing money? Aren't these separate Capital Actions? Yes, there is an argument to be made for that. However, when taking a higher-level view, it is clear that these are both simply different forms of investing.

One might argue that saving money in a bank is a separate Capital Action, but it is still an investment since we deposit our money and earn interest from it. Even keeping cash under a mattress is a kind of invest-ment; it implies that we believe that having physical cash will be more valuable in the future compared to the opportunity cost of investing it elsewhere where it can be lost or become unavailable in times of need. This is common when people don't have faith that they can withdraw their money from a bank when they need it.

Even borrowing money is a form of investing. This is the action of taking on personal risk with someone else's money in the hope and expectation that the money you've borrowed will be less valuable than the result of its use in the future. Think about a mortgage. The expecta-tion is that the house's value will exceed the amount borrowed and interest cost.

CAPITAL OUTCOMES

Now, let's examine the outcomes of these Capital Actions. Each outcome has implications for both individuals and the larger world. As described earlier, this could be as simple as receiving an item purchased or as complex as enabling your faith system to spread across the globe.

There are three orders of outcome through which to look at Capital Outcomes, ranging from their immediate effect to those ongoing and seemingly removed from the initial action. There are also three categories of outcomes: access, freedom, or influence.

1. **Access:** Capital can grant us entry to exclusive places, experiences, or individuals that we wouldn't be able to access otherwise. This is like buying a ticket to a sporting event.
2. **Freedom:** Capital allows us to trade our money for someone else's time. This exchange can free us to pursue activities we otherwise wouldn't have the capacity to, such as hiring someone for a task.
3. **Influence:** When others seek access to capital, they are drawn to those who possess it. Whether you are a homeowner needing services or a significant investor, people are continually looking for capital to help grow their ventures and are willing to offer favors or goodwill in exchange for it.

Capital Outcomes can be either direct or indirect. Some appear immediately while others unfold through a series of cause-and-effect relationships. We often describe these as first-, second-, or third-order outcomes depending on how far they extend from the original Capital Action. Thinking about Capital Actions in these terms helps to visualize the ripple effects of each decision and how even small choices can create lasting, generational impact.

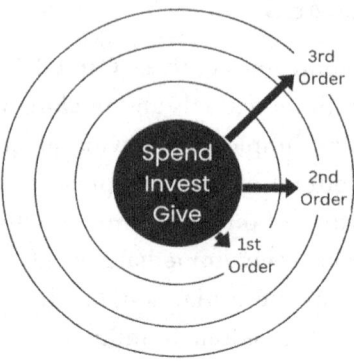

A first-order outcome is an immediate, direct result. This is when you pay for a product and then receive that product.

A second-order outcome is an indirect or follow-on effect that results from the first-order outcome. When you buy a product, you are enabling that company to stay in business, resulting in people keeping their jobs.

A third-order outcome is the ripple effects beyond the second-order effects. This is most often associated with cultural or systemic change. As a result of making the purchase, the company stays in business, and people remain employed, sustaining the local community.

Every Capital Action wields power that the world experiences through first-, second-, and third-order outcomes. Consider the power you are exercising with your Capital Actions.

THE THREE CAPITAL IMPACT FORCES

The most critical question to ask, however, is how are you directing your Capital Actions? If your Capital Actions are driving the outcomes that determine your influence on the world, what is forming those decisions? This brings us to the three Capital Impact Forces: Stewardship, Empowerment, and Alignment.

These are the fundamental forces behind every Capital Action that drive your Capital Outcomes. They are entirely based on your purpose. In fact, they work together to keep your mission driving all of your decisions aligned with your purpose, pushing and pulling each other to provide balance to your decisions.

Stewardship refers to the careful management of finances, while Empowerment emphasizes care for people, and Alignment focuses on commitment to your purpose. These three forces focus on the money, people, and mission, respectively, and how they interact. We will explore each of these concepts in depth in Chapter 4.

Once you start viewing your decisions through this lens, it will become clear how much systems like ESG challenge your mission. When such standards are dictated by an entity that is disconnected from you and your purpose, its interests pull you away from your mission.

But here's the kicker: Even if your interests are perfectly aligned with theirs, your abilities may not seek to serve their entire agenda. In this way, those who are pushing systems that force you away from yours may be more aligned with your Adversary than they are with your purpose! They are seeking to pull the world in a direction aligned with their interests, not yours.

This is why it's so valuable to the common good to pursue your own transcendental purpose.

BUILD YOUR MODEL

We will approach building your model systematically, starting with the most important element: defining your purpose and subsequent mission. In Chapter 4, we'll examine mission alignment and the three Capital Impact Forces, not only what they are but also how you can incorporate them to strengthen your mission.

In Chapter 5, we will discuss Exclusions, specifically the things you need to avoid to stay aligned with your purpose.

Chapter 6 will focus on the positive aspect. If you want to see more specific outcomes in the world, how can you leverage your financial resources to achieve that?

In Chapter 7, we will explore how to decide whether to spend, invest, or give in a certain area, along with how to determine the right Capital Actions to take. This process will involve diligence and discernment.

Finally, Chapter 8 will address how to continually assess and monitor each of these Capital Actions based on the outcomes you observe, along with strategies for engaging with those outcomes and pivoting as necessary.

CHAPTER 3
YOUR PURPOSE.
YOUR MISSION

If our goal is to direct our capital toward genuine virtue in the pursuit
of the good, the true, and the beautiful, it begins with a clear understanding
of our purpose—the reason we exist and the good we seek to advance.

Your mission embodies the enduring purpose that outlines why you or your organization exists. We can express this in various ways, but fundamentally, we all have values that shape our lives and the entities we create.

We understand that when our values align, we sense peace. The Purpose Switch lights up in our brains. Conversely, when they are misaligned, something feels off, and we dislike that sense of missing something. We experience capital confusion. Therefore, having a clearly defined and written purpose holds immense value for us.

This principle applies to both individuals and organizations. Drawing from my nonprofit experience, I've witnessed the importance of mission in a profound way. Nonprofits may strive for financial support, but their core existential purpose is to fulfill their mission. Money is merely fuel needed to accomplish some part of that. This central focus can sometimes get lost in businesses and, even more so, in our personal lives.

We can easily lose sight of our sense of purpose if we haven't clearly defined it. Our purpose is not merely a future aspiration. Instead, it is intrinsic, a fundamental part of who we are, a collection of our values.

NEWMAN'S OWN: FROM SALAD DRESSING TO MISSION-DRIVEN

Paul Newman never intended to change the world with salad dressing. In 1982, the Hollywood legend just enjoyed mixing up batches of his homemade vinaigrette in the basement of his home and giving bottles away to friends and neighbors. But then people started asking for more. A lot more.

Newman's writing partner, A. E. Hotchner, suggested they bottle it commercially. Newman's response was classic: "Let's give all the profits away. It'll be a great joke on everybody." They called it "shameless exploitation for the common good."

What started as a joke became something bigger. The first year, Newman's Own made $300,000 in profit. All of it went to charity, as promised. But the company grew. They added new items: pasta sauce, popcorn, and lemonade. Newman realized that something profound was happening. He wasn't just running a food company anymore. He was stewarding capital for a greater purpose.

Those early years were chaotic. Money flowed to hundreds of different causes: children's charities, environmental groups, disaster relief, arts programs. It felt good to give, but Newman started asking harder questions. Were they actually making a difference, or were they just spreading money around to feel virtuous?

The turning point came in the late 1980s when Newman visited one of the camps his foundation supported. He met kids who had been coming for years, kids whose lives had been genuinely transformed by sustained investment rather than one-time donations. That's when he understood the difference between charitable giving and mission-driven impact.

The company developed clear priorities. Children's and youth programs became the primary focus. They moved from reactive giving to proactive partnership. Instead of writing checks, they built relationships.

They didn't just fund camps. They created the Hole in the Wall Gang Camp network, specifically designed for children with serious illnesses.

By the time of Newman's death in 2008, Newman's Own had donated over $300 million. But more importantly, they had created sustainable programs that continued to grow and multiply their impact. The Hole in the Wall camps alone had served over 1.3 million children and families worldwide.

Newman's transformation from Hollywood star to mission-driven entrepreneur wasn't accidental. It followed a clear pattern: He started with good intentions, then he felt the confusion of unfocused giving, and finally, he discovered the power of aligned purpose.

Newman's Own became a system where every business decision was filtered through a single question: Does this advance our mission to help children thrive?

Newman's "great joke" had become one of the most successful purpose-driven enterprises in history. It is a great example of the power of Purpose-Driven Capital.

ROWING IN THE SAME DIRECTION

Newman's Own became a very public face for a mission forming around true need. When there is no focus, it is easy to turn to anything that feels right in the moment. It is common to suffer from some version of "shiny object syndrome." However, when we commit ourselves to our purpose and our mission, it becomes our driving force.

This driving force compels us to take actions aligned with the life and organizational paths we choose. Our purpose should serve as the foundation for all our plans and decisions, providing cohesion and alignment so that all our actions work in the same direction, just like a team of rowers in a single boat.

I remember my crew days in college. The synchronization of our rowing was the key to our success.

I'll never forget the Austin regatta my freshman year. We were on pace for one of our best times. None of us in the four-man boat had met before the season, so we were still getting to know each other. As this was our third major race together, we were just getting a feel for each other's personalities and strengths. You can imagine the boats: Four men rowing backwards, each of us with one oar on one side of the boat. If one side were rowing stronger than the other, we would either veer off course or have to use the rudder, which would work against our efforts.

We had just reached the point where we could row in sync with each other, and we felt really good about our chances to place in this race. I had a lot of energy that day. The problem was that it was artificial energy. I had been out late the previous night and needed a little pick-me-up. A teammate offered me an energy drink, which I gladly accepted.

I did great for about two-thirds of the race. Then I hit a wall. My energy just went away. Suddenly, I was out of sync, and I felt it. Crab!

A "crab" is when the oar gets caught awkwardly in the water. It was bad. The oar was almost entirely under the boat. Everyone grunted with exhaustion and frustration. The boat started to turn and almost came to a halt. We had to regain our momentum and rhythm just to finish the race. We still had a good race, but unfortunately, we didn't place as we had hoped.

It only took one person rowing out of sync to disrupt our medal-pace. We all responded to the coxswain's commands, rowing in unison, but when my oar got stuck in the water, the entire boat felt the impact. Everyone experienced the discomfort of *that* misalignment.

A mission acts like a coxswain, ensuring that our efforts are directed toward the same goal, the purpose, allowing us to successfully complete our mission, the race. This has been deeply ingrained in me since my time rowing. Because we all knew what we were supposed to be doing, the coxswain was able to guide us all back into our unified rhythm to finish the race.

WHY ALIGNMENT MATTERS: A STUDY ON SOFTWARE TEAMS

Imagine two software teams in the same company. Both are full of smart, capable engineers. Both teams have the same tools, resources, and deadlines, yet one is thriving, meeting deadlines, building trust, and enjoying its work, while the other is stuck, frustrated, finger-pointing, and missing goals.

Why?

The answer isn't talent. It isn't funding. It isn't even management style. It's team alignment.

A group of researchers set out to understand why some software organizations consistently thrive while others struggle. They interviewed engineers and managers across seven companies and surveyed 184 employees to measure one key thing: Are the team's personal values aligned with the company's mission and leadership's priorities?

Their results are fascinating. Aligned teams were more effective and happier, and members trusted each other more. Misaligned teams, however, weren't just a little worse off. They were less effective, less satisfied, and far more likely to experience conflict and distrust.

In fact, one engineer on one of the misaligned teams described it as "rowing in different directions while someone on the shore shouts where they think we're going."[1]

If you want your capital to produce extraordinary outcomes, it must flow where your mission and values are aligned with your actions. Having a clear purpose is a huge asset. As we'll discuss in the next chapter, that's the importance of ensuring that each of your Capital Impact Forces is in sync with your purpose.

THE UNIFIED PURPOSE OF THE TIM TEBOW FOUNDATION AND FAMILY OFFICE

One person who exemplifies mission alignment is Tim Tebow. While he is widely recognized as a world-renowned athlete, in recent years, he has transformed his life into a deeply public mission with a clear purpose. Known as a Heisman Trophy winner from the University of Florida, he made headlines in the 2009 National Championship game by wearing eye black with the Bible verse John 3:16. He was unafraid to express his faith openly.

His teammates, community, and family were all aware of his beliefs, but this public display significantly propelled him into the spotlight that led many Christians to identify with him. For many, Tim became associated with sharing Christian values, using his platform to advocate for various pro-life initiatives, and acting as a strong spokesperson within that community.

As he transitioned into the NFL, he gained fame, wealth, and an extensive following, enjoying all the benefits that come with being a celebrity athlete. He could have chosen a life of luxury. He had the financial resources and access to live almost any life he wanted and even donate to organizations that supported his initiatives and passions.

Tim chose something bigger.

Tim came from a deeply Christian family, a family of missionaries. He wanted to use his platform and resources to fulfill his life's mission. Consequently, he and his wife, Demi-Leigh, chose to commit their time and resources to the Tim Tebow Foundation, focusing on what he has defined as the "MVPs," the Most Vulnerable People. He has a clear definition of the people he aspires to serve.

To support this purpose, he started a family office. This investment firm is not only aligned with the Foundation; it is also designed to build a portfolio that grows in wealth while supporting Tim and his wife's purpose.

It is one of the most remarkable purpose-aligned efforts I've seen. The foundation is supported by the family office, which aims to direct funds as directly as possible to people in need.

Tim's work also encourages others to join in this mission. Every moment of his life is dedicated to considering how he can help more MVPs. He speaks publicly about this commitment and has written extensively on the subject. He feels a profound sense of mission to help these individuals, lamenting the need to take days or even hours to rest.

He regards every moment as an opportunity to assist one more person, advocate for one more individual, or share more of his time, resources, and talents. Tim and Demi-Leigh tirelessly devote their energy to this mission. Their mission statement clearly articulates their purpose, and it remains steadfast.

Through both the foundation and the family office, he and Demi-Leigh strive to bring faith, hope, and love to those in their darkest hours. Their primary focuses include stopping human trafficking and child exploitation, providing orphan care and prevention, addressing profound medical needs, and supporting special needs ministry.

YOUR ADVERSARY WANTS YOU TO LACK CLEAR PURPOSE

Your Adversary's greatest advantage is your lack of clarity about why you exist. Without a clear Purpose Statement and mission, every financial decision becomes a reaction rather than a strategic choice.

Your Adversary wants you to drift through life, making financial choices based on convenience, social pressure, or even short-term emotion rather than long-term purpose. They want you to think purpose clarity is optional.

Their strategy is to keep you so busy with urgent tasks that you never pause to consider your purpose. They want you to believe that defining your purpose is selfish, impractical, or unnecessarily complicated.

So, what does your Adversary fear you'll do? They fear that you'll take the time to clarify what you actually believe and want to accomplish. That you'll write it down, make it specific, and use it to guide your financial decisions.

Having a clear Purpose Statement is like a GPS for your capital. You're driving around in circles without it, but with it, every decision has direction. Your Adversary needs you to be lost, but your purpose points to your true north.

MISSION MIS-IDENTITY

Unless you clearly define your purpose and direct your mission toward it, your efforts may fall short. Your purpose serves as your "why" to guide your mission and its actions. Your capital, then, becomes the fuel that supports that mission.

However, if your mission is lacking, it can create problems. There's dissonance; something feels off. Just as a map loses its purpose without a destination, a mission is incomplete if you're not fully living it. A life or organization without a clear purpose and mission can lead to unnecessary challenges and lost opportunities to create something greater. The Purpose Switch is inactive, and capital confusion kicks in. You may waste time, energy, and opportunities.

This disconnect can create tension from inconsistent and clashing values, leading to stress, rationalization, and even regret when you realize later on that you haven't been true to your mission. Psychologically speaking, this can manifest as cognitive dissonance, where your values clash with your actions.

This can make you feel that you're not living up to your ideal self. You might also experience moral disengagement, where you justify unethical behavior because "everyone else does it." This can lead to self-discrepancy, where the loss of a clear self-identity occurs, and potentially moral licensing, where you convince yourself that your past good deeds excuse your current lapses in values. These patterns can lead to unhappiness, cynicism, a weakened moral compass, and even a loss of inner peace.

While it manifests differently at individual and organizational levels, the absence of a clear purpose in a business leads to wasted time, energy, and opportunities. This results in a conflict of values, especially when two people within the organization are pursuing different goals. This can even extend to decision-makers.

For instance, if two executives have opposing views, one advocating for option A and the other for option B, deciding on a course of action is challenging without a shared set of values. This situation can lead to feelings of stress, rationalization, and regret, all of which affect the organization as a whole. If you find yourself asking, "How did we get into this mess?" it's often because a decision was made without a clear foundation or rationale behind it.

This mindset can also apply to other social efforts. Organizations might justify unethical behaviors by attempting to offset them with a single good action. They might think, *We are doing all these morally questionable things in our business, but we'll balance it out by investing our efforts in some other good initiatives.* These initiatives may include seeking strong ESG ratings, giving to charities that counteract their bad practices, or engaging in public campaigns that encourage doing as I say, not as I do.

While this approach seems like the opposite of moral licensing, it operates under a similar principle. Organizations frequently engage in this behavior, which can create a sense of moral guilt within them.

A lack of a clear purpose grounded in values often lies at the heart of this issue. Even if an organization has a defined mission statement, it may not align with its core values, leading to these discrepancies.

WITH PURPOSE COMES JOY

Having a clear purpose brings passion and purpose to your life because it creates the conditions for your Purpose Switch to activate consistently. When you know your purpose and see your financial decisions advancing it, you experience the neurological satisfaction that comes from values-aligned behavior.

A written Purpose Statement provides your brain the clarity needed to recognize alignment versus misalignment in your daily choices. Without a clearly defined purpose, your Purpose Switch loses its objective footholds and can't engage effectively. You might feel vaguely uncomfortable about certain purchases or investments, but it may be difficult to identify why or what to do about it.

With purpose clarity, every financial decision becomes an opportunity for Purpose Switch activation when you choose correctly or uncomfortable feedback when your choices drift from your stated values. The Purpose Statement transforms abstract values into concrete decision-making criteria that your brain can process and reward

CRAFTING YOUR PURPOSE STATEMENT

Oftentimes, we have a good sense of our purpose, but we don't have the words for it. If you or your organization falls into that category, you may want to consider crafting a Purpose Statement.

So, what is a Purpose Statement? It is very much like a mission statement, but with a key philosophical difference. Your mission statement focuses on what you do. Your Purpose Statement focuses on WHY you exist.

This can be created for either private family/individual use or for organizations. However, it is difficult to stress the importance of being able to consistently express, as Simon Sinek elegantly brought into our lexicon, your "why."

Each of us has unique charisms, gifts, perspectives, and bank account balances. However, we get to use these to make an impact on the world, providing benefit to ourselves and others in a way that nobody else can. As a result we each have a distinct and unique purpose.

You must know your Purpose Statement. That's why I recommend putting it in writing. Post it somewhere prominent so that you won't forget it. You get to decide if it is public or private. The one thing you can't do is forget it.

Unlike mission statements, which are typically living statements that usually evolve over time, a Purpose Statement expresses your enduring reason for being. Core principles and values don't change.

Here's a systematic approach you can take to define your Purpose Statement. Although you may want to develop your own formula, this approach provides an easy starting point for examining and thinking through it from a "purpose lens."

Step one: Reflect on your core values. Identify five to ten values that drive you.

- What do I and/or my organization want to be known or remembered for?
- When have I felt most aligned and most conflicted?
- What do I feel most passionate about?

Family, social issues, business, impact, faith? Make a list of the five to ten core values you can identify based on your answers to these questions.

Step two: Define your ultimate purpose.

- Why am I here?
- What do I feel like I'm being called to in this life?
- What eternal or legacy goals am I pursuing?
- What do I hope to be remembered for?
- What do I want to leave for the next generation?
- What kind of world do I want to help create?

Try to refine those into a common vision, perhaps encapsulating it into a single sentence that holds meaning for you.

Step three: Inventory your gifts and resources.

- What are the various areas where you can offer something unique? It can be financial, including your income, assets, bank holdings, and future expectations.
- How about your relational resources? Family, friends, your faith community, business networks, partnerships, etc. Who do you know that can help you or help others?

Now, think about the unique gifts that you have: your knowledge base, unique skills, and experience. What have you learned individually or organizationally that brings value to others? Everybody is seeking these things, but this is something that's unique to you. What wisdom have you gained?

Step four: Clarify the impact you want to have.

- Who are you called to serve?
- What stirs your passion?
- Is there anything that you want to follow, pursue, grow, impact, or become a part of?
- What do you feel can be uniquely accomplished through your life?

Step five: Draft Your Purpose Statement

Your Purpose Statement is one clear sentence that captures the reason you exist. It's not about what you do. It's about why it matters. When you write it down, it will feel almost uncomfortably simple, but that's what makes it powerful. It brings into focus that which you know and forces you to acknowledge that as the core of why you make choices you do.

Here is a simple framework:

Our purpose is to [*verb or impact*] [*audience or sphere*] so that [*transcendent outcome*].

Here are two fictional examples using this formula:

Legacy Harvest Foods: *"Our purpose is to nourish families and restore creation so that thriving communities reflect care for our shared home."*

Fictional Family Office: *"Our purpose is to steward our family's wealth wisely so that our family can continue to help the world around us flourish and strive toward virtue."*

Here are some real-world examples of mission statements that read like Purpose Statements:

Patagonia: *"We exist to inspire and implement solutions to the environmental crisis by using our business, resources, and profits to protect and preserve nature in order to leave the world better for future generations."*

Lego Group: *"Inspire and develop the builders of tomorrow."*

John Maxwell: "Every day, I add value to leaders who multiply value to others."

Tom Monaghan: "My mission is to use the talents and resources God has entrusted to me to advance the Catholic faith and build institutions that form future leaders."

Your Purpose Statement should be a guiding light for you and illuminate all steps laid out throughout this book as you continue to think through the framework and develop yours.

THE POWER OF A PURPOSE IN DAILY LIFE

A clearly stated purpose paints a path toward alignment. It enables daily actions that reflect your beliefs, provides ethical clarity, and ensures that you are striving for legacy-driven impact, so it may be helpful to keep it front of mind every day. Put it in a place of prominence.

Your financial decisions have an impact. Having a clearly stated purpose enables you and your organization to pursue your mission with the greatest possible force, using your capital in pursuit of its highest and best purpose.

CHAPTER 4
PURPOSE ALIGNMENT AND THE CAPITAL IMPACT FORCES

If our goal is to direct capital toward genuine virtue in the pursuit of the good, the true, and the beautiful, it is critical to harness the forces of Stewardship, Empowerment, and Alignment, all anchored by our unique purpose.

MISSION-ALIGNED MIRACLE ON THE HUDSON

On January 15, 2009, US Airways Flight 1549 took off from New York's LaGuardia Airport. Nobody expected anything out of the ordinary. Just minutes into the flight, disaster struck. A flock of geese flew into both engines, disabling them completely. The plane was only at 3,000 feet. It was too low to turn back and too far to glide to another airport.

Captain Chesley Burnett "Sully" Sullenberger immediately communicated with air traffic control to let them know his plan. Just a few moments later, he realized he was out of options. He had never encountered a situation like this in his forty-two years of flying, but it was one of thousands of situations he had already visualized. After 19,000 hours of flying experience and seven years in the Air Force, he knew exactly what he had to do.

Against standard protocol, he took control of the aircraft from First Officer Jeff Skiles. Then he calmly reported to air traffic control, "We're gonna be in the Hudson."

Sully realized that the plane would not make it back to land. Now he had a new mission: Save the lives of all 155 souls on board. As one of the most experienced pilots in the country, he made the decision that would be most likely to lead to that outcome.

"This is the captain. Brace for impact."

He alerted air control, knowing that they would send emergency crews to their location immediately. He knew what his crew was trained to do when he said "brace for impact," and they prepared necessary emergency procedures.

Every decision made, almost entirely on instinct, was guided toward his one and only mission. And on that day, his mission was accomplished. All 155 people survived.

This feat was considered so extraordinary that it has been called the Miracle on the Hudson. This outcome could not have been achieved if decisions had not aligned with the mission.

Had Sully tried to reach an airport to avoid a water landing, he wouldn't have made it. Had the flight attendants not initiated emergency procedures to evacuate passengers from the plane in an orderly manner, some people might not have made it.

This miracle was accomplished because of a unified, mission-driven effort, but the outcome could have been very different if preparations had not been made for such extraordinary circumstances. Sully was able to adapt the mission to serve his purpose as the pilot.

RESOURCES, PEOPLE, PURPOSE

It is amazing what can be accomplished when everyone is pursuing a common mission. While the Miracle on the Hudson was not a financial action, it illustrates the principles behind making mission-aligned financial decisions that lead to your desired outcome.

To do this, we first need to consider what drives our mission. Generally, it's influenced by three independent forces: resources, people, and purpose.

These three themes are common across many disciplines. However, in the context of the Purpose-Driven Capital Framework, they are instrumental for achieving Capital Outcomes that align with our mission. As we discussed, the three Capital Impact Forces guide the Capital Actions, which result in Capital Outcomes. Each of these forces should pursue the virtues outlined by our mission.

When companies are well aligned, they tend to perform better overall. Studies indicate that such companies experience 50 percent faster revenue growth, 72 percent higher profitability, 16 percent greater customer satisfaction, and 30 percent more employee engagement than their misaligned counterparts.[1] This data highlights that purpose and mission alignment unites everyone in the organization, from top leadership to all team members, and even those they serve. Mission alignment drives satisfaction of organizations and individuals alike.

Establishing a purpose-driven structure leads to significant outcomes for both organizations and individuals.

YOUR ADVERSARY WANTS YOUR PURPOSE DISCONNECTED

Your Adversary understands that even people with a clear purpose fail to connect that purpose to their financial decisions. They want you to compartmentalize, separating your values from your money.

So, what does your Adversary want? Put simply, they want you to see your purpose as something separate from your financial life. They want you to think that Stewardship, Empowerment, and Alignment are nice concepts that don't apply to real-world money decisions... and certainly shouldn't be considered for every Capital Action.

Your Adversary's strategy is to convince you that integrating your values with your finances is impractical, inefficient, or, of course, financially costly. They want you to believe that you can pursue your purpose through volunteer work and passive donations while your money works against your mission.

So, what does your Adversary fear you'll do? They fear that you'll recognize the power of aligning the three Capital Impact Forces toward a unified purpose to create extraordinary outcomes.

Your Adversary needs these forces to oppose each other. When Stewardship, Empowerment, and Alignment work together, they create something especially powerful: capital that compounds your mission direction.

THE THREE FORCES TAKING FLIGHT

For an airplane to successfully fulfill its purpose, it needs three fundamental controls to fly and reach its destination: the throttle, the yoke, and the rudder. The throttle controls engine power, giving the plane the energy it needs to lift and move forward. The yoke controls pitch and roll, allowing the pilot to steer and orient the aircraft. The rudder keeps the aircraft aligned, ensuring that it stays balanced and on course, particularly in times of turbulence or crosswinds. Without any of these controls, the flight is compromised, becoming directionless, unstable, or powerless.

The Purpose Driven Capital model relies on the coordinated functioning of the three Capital Impact Forces: Stewardship, Empowerment, and Alignment.

- **Stewardship is like the throttle.** It manages and fuels our capital, ensuring we have sufficient fuel to reach our destination at the right speed.
- **Empowerment is like the yoke.** It ensures our capital serves others and moves with intention.
- **Alignment is like the rudder.** It keeps our decisions in sync with our core purpose and values, particularly in times when our purpose is challenged.

Just like a flight, all three of these controls are needed to get to the destination, to accomplish the mission that fulfills its purpose. When any one of the three is off, the destination/purpose may take more effort to reach—if it is even possible to reach it at all.

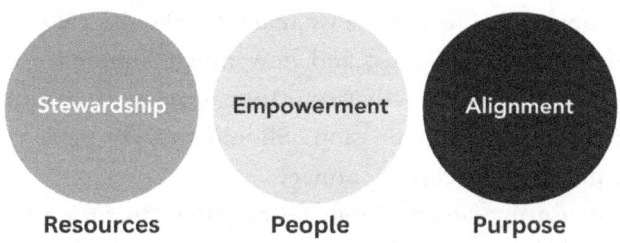

Each of the three Capital Impact Forces focuses on one component: your resources, people, or purpose. Stewardship focuses on managing resources responsibly; Empowerment is centered around people, and Alignment connects directly to our overarching purpose. These three components are interrelated and must be viewed together rather than in isolation. Based on their dynamics, they influence every Capital Action.

STEWARDSHIP

Let's begin with Stewardship, which is the disciplined management of resources to maximize long-term mission impact while maintaining financial stability: "How can I use this money most effectively for my purpose over time?"

Stewardship is the power behind your Capital Actions. In the airplane, this is represented by the thrust generated by the throttle. In a cockpit, this is the lever that is pushed forward. The further forward you push it, the more fuel is used to create more speed or climb higher.

Stewardship involves the responsible management and care of resources to achieve long-term financial goals. This means managing financial assets not just for immediate gain but with future benefits in mind. For instance, I may consider spending money now, but that decision might sacrifice future purchases. Conversely, if I save for future goals, I might forego immediate desires. Each decision requires careful consideration of how to best use financial resources in alignment with our purpose.

We also need to assess our financial return expectations. Do we need rapid growth, or can we afford to wait? What's the time horizon for our investment? Should it span days, years, or even generations? Risk tolerance is another critical factor: are we ready to take risks with our money for potentially greater returns, and how much liquidity do we need? Both of these also relate directly to our time horizon. How much time do we have to accomplish our mission? Should we take more risk now to potentially increase our capital sooner?

If I must use my current financial resources to support my family, that money must remain readily accessible, i.e., liquid. However, if I have sufficient funds for immediate needs, I could invest some of that money in ventures that grow over time, without needing immediate access.

EMPOWERMENT

Next, we turn to Empowerment, which ensures that your capital serves human dignity and creates opportunities for yourself or others to flourish. It asks, "How does this money serve people in a way that honors their dignity and potential?"

If you'll recall, Empowerment is like the yoke. In an airplane cockpit, this is the steering wheel or stick. This is what a pilot uses to pitch and roll, pointing the nose of the plane up and down or rolling the plane side to side to turn. It guides the plane to its destination.

Empowerment involves creating opportunities for ourselves or others to grow, thrive, and succeed, giving them the power, autonomy, and responsibility to achieve their goals. This could mean helping someone secure their daily needs, supporting a leader in uplifting an entire community, or providing someone with the means to escape poverty.

When empowering others, we must consider a few key factors: Who are we supporting? Are they aligned with our mission and values? What are our relationships with these individuals, and what do our partnerships mean in this context? Additionally, we must acknowledge our self-interest. Like the oxygen mask in an airplane, we have to take care of ourselves first to ensure that we can continue supporting others.

While pursuing our goals, it's important to recognize that our actions can't be entirely self-interested. We all bear some responsibility for others, which raises the question of how much capital or resources we should commit to help them.

ALIGNMENT

From the concept of Empowerment, we then move to the third force impacting capital: Alignment. Alignment ensures that your Capital Actions remain consistent with your deepest values and purpose, especially when facing pressure or turbulence. Essentially, it means asking, "Does this choice reflect my/our identity and who I am/we are called to be?"

In the plane analogy, this is the rudder, which affects the yaw, the side-to-side movement of the flight. If you've ever seen a plane landing in a headwind, this is what keeps the plane on course even when the flight looks like it is landing at a forty-five-degree angle compared to the runway. The rudder ensures that the flight moves in the right direction, despite the wind's influence. In the cockpit, it's controlled by the foot pedals the pilot uses.

In terms of the Capital Impact Forces, Alignment is the consistency of your purpose and mission with respect to your values. Our spending choices reflect our desires for the kind of world we want to see. Where we allocate our money indicates what we want to see more of in the world.

COMPLEMENTARY FORCES

These three forces are not meant to be isolated. They work together, and each of them has a direct impact on the others. This can be illustrated with the Venn diagram below.

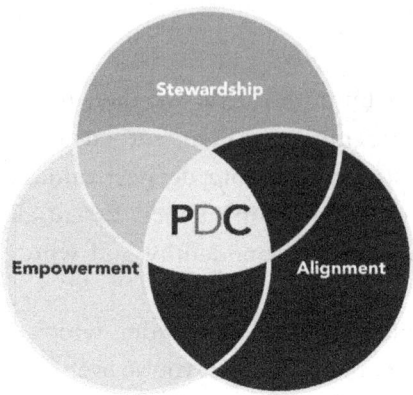

The Stewardship circle is on top. It intersects with Alignment on the lower right. Stewardship and Alignment intersect with the Empowerment circle in the lower left side. In the middle, where they all intersect, is where you will achieve Purpose-Driven Capital.

The balance of Purpose-Driven Capital is based on your purpose and how you define each of the Capital Impact Forces for your Capital Actions. You will know that you have accurately defined each of them when you see that the perfect intersection of these three forces directly points to your purpose and mission.

Each force has a particular direction and interest. What happens when those interests compete against each other for the same resources or efforts?

PUSH AND PULL: COMPETING FORCES

While the three Capital Impact Forces should function together seamlessly, they have naturally competing interests. While Stewardship focuses on controlling funds, whether preserving or growing them, Empowerment aims to benefit people, and Alignment seeks to strengthen the mission, potentially leading to tensions between these priorities. For instance, if I'm hungry, an expensive meal nearby may seem like the best immediate solution, but it might not be the optimal long-term use of funds or in service to my purpose for the money I'm stewarding.

Each of these interests operates independently and may not align until we intentionally make them work together. Finding common ground among these forces is vital to achieving our ultimate goals.

We can think of the three Capital Impact Forces as having a healthy tension that is designed to give them strength. Take concrete, for example. You know that concrete is always poured on a mesh of thick steel bars. The steel is called rebar, and it is absolutely necessary for the concrete to function.

Concrete is incredibly strong under compression but terribly weak under tension. In other words, concrete is extremely strong when subjected to weight, but it becomes brittle and breaks when subjected to forces that pull or bend it. The rebar provides the necessary tensile strength, resisting such pulling and bending forces.

You can imagine that kind of dynamic working between the three Capital Impact Forces.

BALANCING THE TENSION

No matter how much we want to help others, doing so always requires additional resources. We need to find a balance; there's a tension between the continuous need for assistance and the availability of funds that could be directed toward helping people. However, we must ask ourselves, "Is that the best and highest use of the money?"

The answer may vary depending on the situation. For example, when considering Stewardship in relation to our purpose, we always strive to serve our purpose, whether we are helping people or growing a large company. Whatever that mission is, there is a cost associated with fulfilling it. Moreover, this mission is never truly complete; we are continually aware that there is more to accomplish.

This leads us to a scenario where, between Empowerment and Alignment, we may find people with whom it makes financial sense to engage but who don't necessarily align with our purpose. Sometimes, the values they represent may conflict with our goals, creating potential clashes.

STEWARDSHIP <> EMPOWERMENT

Let's explore the intersection of Stewardship and Empowerment. In this conflict, Stewardship pushes for maximum efficiency and returns, while Empowerment calls for serving people who may not be "efficient" enough. While Empowerment requires careful Stewardship, there is a corresponding strength that arises from these two elements working in harmony rather than against each other. If both aspects are aligned with the purpose, they can create a more potent force.

A good example of this tension is an organization offering scholarships. From the perspective of Stewardship, they should logically award scholarships to students with the highest GPAs and other indicators of success. These students would be most likely to succeed and reflect well on the issuer of the scholarship. However, Empowerment would like to see scholarships go to students with the greatest need. They may struggle more, but they would also benefit most from the opportunity to go to school without the burden of that expense. This healthy tension may result in criteria that consider both academic potential and financial or socioeconomic need.

STEWARDSHIP <> ALIGNMENT

At the intersection of Stewardship and Alignment, we find that financial decisions must keep the mission in mind. The conflict between these two is that Stewardship focuses on preserving and growing resources, while Alignment insists on staying true to values even when costly. A promising investment opportunity may arise, but if it doesn't align with our mission, it is unlikely to succeed. If both Stewardship and Alignment can work collaboratively, they will help advance our mission.

Conversely, Stewardship might indicate that while there's a fantastic opportunity to serve the mission, we currently lack the necessary resources. It may not be wise to pursue that opportunity right now due to resource constraints.

We may see this when considering a potential business partnership. Stewardship may encourage the partnership because the other company is highly profitable and would allow you to expand your business.

However, the Alignment force may alert you to the fact that their business practices contradict your mission. The resolution to this would be to set criteria for partners that factor in both the size and capability of the business, as well as the values that align with your mission.

EMPOWERMENT <> ALIGNMENT

Empowerment ensures that our mission supports people, not just the end goal, which often puts it in conflict with Alignment. While Empowerment aims to support everyone, Alignment emphasizes maintaining a focused mission and staying within its scope. There may be specific outcomes we wish to achieve, but if those do not benefit the people involved, it will likely be counterproductive. The tension between these two forces empowers us to direct our efforts appropriately toward the mission. When our focus is on the mission, the tensions between these factors can often find relief.

This may become apparent when hiring someone. The Empowerment force may be pulling you to hire a person who desperately needs a job, regardless of their abilities. However, the Alignment force may pull you back to your mission and ensure that the company is staffed with competent people who can fulfill its purpose. There are many ways to resolve this, but one suggestion may be to offer more entry-level positions to those who are less prepared for the role but are still capable of contributing.

Often, we need to discern which force is dominant. If resources are insufficient to support the people, the financial stewardship aspect may take precedence in decision-making. This tension can manifest across all three Capital Impact Forces. The decision will come down to your purpose, your mission. While there may be tension between the forces, when you are focused on your purpose, resolution is much easier to recognize because it typically strikes a balance between the two forces.

THE TIM TEBOW FOUNDATION: CAPITAL IMPACT FORCES

Let's take a look at the Tim Tebow Foundation, which we discussed earlier regarding its strong mission focus. They work hand-in-hand with The Tebow Group, their family office investment arm. They have clearly defined their three Capital Impact Forces within their mission. In terms of Stewardship, they leverage their brand in the community and make investments that directly support their philanthropic goals. As for Empowerment, they focus on their most vulnerable populations while also recognizing the businesses that contribute to this support. In terms of Alignment, their Christian values, rooted in faith, hope, and love, are integral to every program, from partner selection to execution.

BALANCING THE TENSION: BUYING A HOME

Let's use an example to illustrate this concept: buying a house. While some might view purchasing a home as spending, most would agree that buying a home is, in fact, an investment action. The capital outcomes of this decision include homeownership, providing a safe space for the family, and granting the previous owner financial compensation.

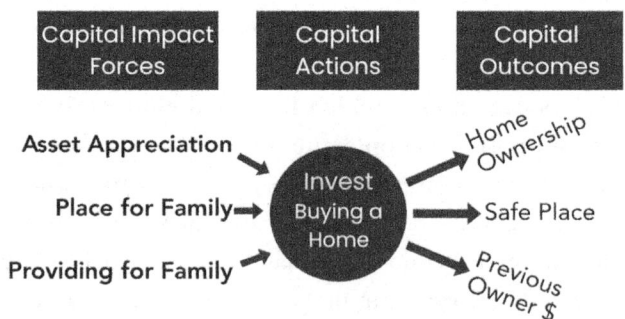

But what Capital Impact Forces influenced this choice? From a Stewardship perspective, owning a home allows for asset appreciation as opposed to you having to continuously pay rent, which supports someone else's investment.

From an Empowerment standpoint, buying a home creates a nurturing environment for your family, offering them a place to thrive. Moreover, from a perspective of Alignment, if your mission is to take care of your family and lead them to a better situation than your current one, providing a safe home plays a significant role in fulfilling that mission.

These various influences guided the decision to purchase the home, allowing for personal ownership, safety for the family, and even benefiting the community by providing a return on investment to the previous homeowner.

The three Capital Impact Forces—Stewardship, Empowerment, and Alignment—work together to create favorable Capital Outcomes, making Capital Action decisions easier. When these forces are considered collectively, decisions can be made more effectively and consistently, facilitating desired outcomes.

Understanding your purpose is foundational. By applying these three Capital Impact Forces to your purpose, you can achieve the outcomes you wish to see. This process starts with recognizing these forces, enabling you to make informed decisions regarding Capital Actions.

ENTERING PART II

To effectively guide our Capital Actions, we need to identify and exclude problematic actions while prioritizing purpose-aligned initiatives. The forces influencing capital impact will inevitably lead to certain outcomes, but we must establish a clear framework for each action that goes beyond just observation.

The Exclusions involve Capital Actions that contradict our mission, ethics, or morals, or that lead to negative outcomes. Conversely, our Elevations focus on capital priorities that advance our purpose without compromising our ethical standards.

This moves us into Part II, where we will objectively evaluate what you must avoid to stay aligned with your purpose and what will enhance your mission. We will discuss the Exclusions in Chapter 5 and the Elevations in Chapter 6.

PART TWO
GUIDE YOUR OUTCOMES

PART TWO

CHAPTER 5
EXCLUSIONS: WHAT TO ELIMINATE

If our goal is to direct our capital toward genuine virtue in the pursuit of the good, the true, and the beautiful, it is necessary to eliminate anything that actively opposes those things. This is the importance of Exclusions.

BUFFETT'S CHALLENGE

Warren Buffett, widely considered one of the most successful investors in history, once gave a roomful of MBA students an unexpected challenge.

"Imagine you have a punch card with only twenty slots. That's it. Twenty investments for your entire life. Once you fill them, you're done."

The students looked around at each other and laughed nervously. Only twenty? In our lifetimes?

But Buffett doubled down. His point wasn't to create fear. It was to force clarity. If you could only make twenty investment decisions, you'd be far more selective. You wouldn't waste time chasing trends. You'd say no to almost everything, just like he does.

Buffett doesn't start by asking what to invest in. He starts by knowing what he won't invest in. He already knows that he won't invest in companies he doesn't understand, industries with no competitive edge, or management teams he doesn't trust. By narrowing the world through intentional Exclusions, he removes noise, reduces decision fatigue, and stays aligned with his investing mission.

In his case, elimination is a filter that helps him get to his mission faster.

It may seem counterintuitive, but the first step in determining what we want to pursue is to identify what we do not want to engage in. This is where Exclusions come into play. Our Exclusions create boundaries, allowing us to define our playing field, clarify our true intentions, and determine how to allocate our resources effectively.

However, our Purpose-Driven Capital Framework goes a step further. We are not merely seeking to eliminate deals that we don't want to work with. We are eliminating anything that is morally or ethically opposed to our purpose.

TOM MONAGHAN'S PIVOT TO PURPOSE

A great example of this is Tom Monaghan. He is known as the billionaire founder of Domino's Pizza and the "Golden Era" owner of the Detroit Tigers. But that is not how people know him today. He has lived most of his life in the public eye. Few of us have that kind of scrutiny on our decisions, but it was because of this public face that he was confronted with an uncomfortable question that changed the course of his incredible life.

Sitting across from a reporter from a local news station, he responded to questions about Michigan, his business success, and his Catholic philanthropic vision. At the time, Monaghan had everything he ever wanted: mansions, classic cars, a private jet, and even his own major league baseball team. He was living a dream that seemed as distant as the moon for a kid who had risen from a challenging childhood growing up in an orphanage when his parents couldn't handle taking care of him. From the outside, he had achieved the American dream.

Like many who rise from scarcity, his first instinct was to enjoy the fruits of success. He bought luxurious homes and rare cars and indulged in the lifestyle he had always imagined. He was even in the process of building his dream home, designed by legendary architect Frank Lloyd

Wright. He would later reflect that, to that point, he had focused on building wealth and enjoying it.

But there had been a growing tension for a while. His wife lovingly sought to live a humble life and didn't care much for the extravagant one Tom was pursuing. Internally, Monaghan was facing his own inconsistencies. He had been raised Catholic and even gone to seminary, thinking he might be called to be a priest. Only later did he publicly admit that this was a growing challenge for him at this time.

That led to a question he didn't expect, one that would hit so hard it became a turning point for his life. The interview was moving along just like the hundreds, if not thousands, he had done before that. But then the reporter asked, "How do you reconcile your Catholic faith with this lavish lifestyle?"

Monaghan had no good answer. His dramatic pause was filled with introspection.

That question forced Monaghan to rethink his approach to life. He began to methodically evaluate all of his affiliations, particularly his business interests. Much to his daughter's dismay, he sold the Tigers. He sold his rare cars. Eventually, he sold Domino's. More than 90 percent of his wealth would eventually be redirected to serve a mission greater than himself.

So, where do you start when you have access to anything you could ever want to do? Monaghan started with what he could no longer support. He looked at his faith and assessed the most egregious violations. He decided to start by opposing any activities that enabled abortion, pornography, and anti-family practices. All of these violated his conscience, and he knew that if this was true for him, it would be true for others as well.

As a result, he was able to start moving toward his purpose. He eventually helped found Ave Maria Mutual Funds to give others the chance to invest without compromising their beliefs. He built a university, a law school, and an international organization for Catholic leaders. His wealth transformed into a legacy because he chose to align with his purpose.

Tom Monaghan's turning point illustrates a simple truth. Clarity of purpose begins when we decide what no longer belongs.

INTRODUCTION TO EXCLUSIONS

Moral exclusions make allocating our capital significantly easier. We tend to support more things than we are willing to reject, so it is helpful to start with what we can immediately exclude to protect the integrity of our mission.

When considering our exclusions, we should begin with our core beliefs. This is true for individuals as well as organizations. There is always a line you are not willing to cross. How far are you willing to go to accomplish your goals? I guarantee you can think of some boundaries.

For instance, if your mission is to become the most profitable firm in the world, are you willing to rob all of your clients? Banks? The poor? Doing so would unquestionably increase your bottom line, but I have no doubt that you find at least one, if not all, of those reprehensible. That is one of your boundaries.

When it comes to committing capital, people may be unwilling to support many different causes. For some these may include tobacco, alcohol, or gambling. For others it may include predatory lending, fossil fuels, or weapons of mass destruction.

While Buffett has his own unbreakable investment criteria, we all have our own moral and ethical boundaries that we will not cross.

YOUR ADVERSARY WANTS YOUR SUPPORT

Your Adversary doesn't just want you to be passively indifferent. They want your active financial support. They thrive when you fund their operations through your unconscious financial choices.

They want you to assume that your financial choices don't really matter, that the connection between your money and harmful outcomes is too distant to worry about. They want you to prioritize convenience and cost over conscience.

Your Adversary's strategy is simple: They want to make research seem inconvenient and expensive while making their initiatives cheap and easy. They obfuscate unethical practices in complex supply chains and technical jargon. They are betting that you won't dig deeper.

So, what does your Adversary most fear you'll do? That you'll ask the hard questions: "What am I actually funding? Who benefits from my financial choices? What would happen if I demanded transparency?"

When you establish clear exclusions, you're not just avoiding harm. You're making a stand for your beliefs. Your Adversary's business model benefits from your ignorance. Your Exclusions take away their cover.

THE VIRTUE OF MORAL NEUTRALITY

Not every investment needs to be made in pursuit of something higher and greater. In fact, most should not. There's profound virtue in pursuing morally neutral Capital Actions. These are actions that simply pass your Exclusions Screening. In the next chapter, we will discuss Elevations, which often require extra demand to pursue an even greater good in the name of your purpose.

You can think of it this way. If you avoid funding harm and occasionally fund extraordinary good, you will remain on the side of pursuing what is truly good. Just think about how far ahead you will be if you simply avoid that which opposes your values. By not supporting your Adversary, you are still enabling the good.

A diversified stock fund that excludes your non-negotiables but doesn't actively advance your mission is virtuous. Investing in a real estate project with managers who are aligned with your purpose is good.

While it is important to be aware of how our money is used for first-, second-, and third-order outcomes, it is impossible to do that with every Capital Action. The Purpose-Driven Capital Framework isn't about making every dollar a moral crusade. It's about ensuring that your capital never works against your values first. Then you can pursue extraordinary actions when it makes sense and is possible.

Being morally neutral is a challenging pursuit, but one that is extremely worthy of the time and attention it takes. Exclusions are the primary starting point to getting there.

THE PRACTICAL VALUE OF EXCLUSIONS

Exclusions help you make decisions faster and easier. By having a list of exclusions clearly stated, you simplify life for yourself and those aligned with your purpose. Exclusions serve as a quick reference that everyone involved, including you, can rely on to understand your boundaries. This concept acts like a policy that guides your actions.

There are three key benefits to defining your Exclusions:

1. **Clarity:** You gain a clear understanding of where you stand, as everything is documented. This creates well-defined boundaries for your mission.
2. **Speed:** Exclusions empower proactive decision-making and reduce decision fatigue, allowing for quicker resolutions.
3. **Consistency:** Having clear exclusions helps build trust with stakeholders. It signals what matters to you and your mission, reinforcing your integrity.

EXCLUSIONS ATTRACT

Exclusions don't merely simplify decisions; they also safeguard your mission, protect your integrity, and communicate your values with clarity and conviction. Moreover, Exclusions attract others who share your values. This clarity helps you cultivate meaningful relationships and partnerships, as people are naturally drawn to those who demonstrate conviction and establish boundaries.

CREATING YOUR LIST

Exclusions act not just as walls but as welcoming signs for the right individuals. So, how do you determine your list of exclusions? This process can be challenging unless you know where to begin. Here are four key areas to consider when identifying what you stand for and, importantly, what you cannot stand for:

1. **Moral or Theological Reasons:** Your moral compass and values form the foundation of your exclusions. These may stem from a religious belief system or a humanitarian perspective. Look for documents or leaders in these areas that align with your values and help you identify critical issues that require consideration.

2. **Mission or Identity Alignment:** Reflect on your mission and what is necessary to preserve its integrity. Consider any actions or decisions that could contradict your self-perception or the identity of your organization.

3. **Stakeholder and Community Expectations:** Understand the convictions of your internal team and the values of other stakeholders. Identify what is important to them and determine if Exclusions are necessary to support their beliefs.

4. **Legal, Regulatory, and Compliance Risks:** Investigate the laws and industry-specific regulations that may impact your actions. Be aware of your fiduciary duties, along with the regulatory and reputational safeguards you need in place to protect your organization.

You can draw upon your business context and personal values to find the right information for establishing Exclusions within these four categories.

NON-NEGOTIABLE VS. CIRCUMSTANTIAL

Once you create your list based on these categories, assess the two different types of Exclusions that apply to each item.

The first category is non-negotiable, while the second is circumstantial. Non-negotiable Exclusions are those issues with which you are unwilling or unable to compromise under any circumstances. In contrast, circumstantial Exclusions refer to activities where the initial action or resulting outcome might not be significant but could be under certain conditions.

For instance, some examples of non-negotiable exclusions include issues like abortion and pornography for individuals such as Tom

Monaghan. A widely accepted non-negotiable for many, including the Tebow Foundation, is human trafficking. For various organizations, another non-negotiable might be atomic weapons.

Conversely, a circumstantial issue related to human trafficking might be wage suppression, where individuals are underpaid for their work. There are situations where wage suppression might seem reasonable; for example, many believe that minimum wage laws reflect wage suppression because the set minimum is deemed too low based on current standards.

Others might argue that a fourteen-year-old doesn't necessarily need to earn a living wage. Some individuals even view wage suppression as a form of human trafficking, though it is typically not regarded as such.

While atomic weapons are non-negotiable for many, firearms are often not viewed in the same light. Firearms can serve various purposes, including hunting or personal defense, and are not inherently designed for destruction, though they can be used as weapons. Thus, for many, firearms might represent a circumstantial example of this issue.

This assessment affects the weight you place on discerning future decisions. Non-negotiable issues are typically clear-cut, while circumstantial ones may reside in a gray area.

EXCLUSIONS AND THE IMPACT FORCES

Next, let's explore how Exclusions interact with the Capital Impact Forces. Each Exclusion corresponds to one or more impact force. Since these forces need to align and cannot oppose each other, every impact force must aim toward a unified outcome. Compromising any of the impact forces while neglecting the Exclusions will disrupt their alignment, leading to negative actions and outcomes that could be detrimental to your mission.

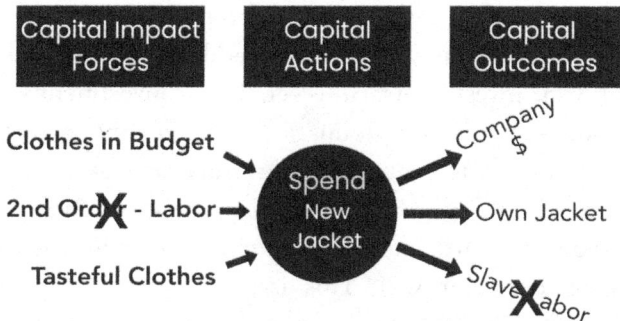

To illustrate this, consider three examples, one for each type of Capital Impact Force. The first example is the purchase of a jacket.

While it may seem innocuous, this spending action has various outcomes, such as first-order outcomes like the company receiving money and you acquiring a new jacket. From a Stewardship standpoint, if the purchase fits within your budget, it is acceptable. If the jacket is tasteful, it aligns with your values. However, if the jacket's production involved slave labor, this raises concerns regarding the Empowerment impact force. By purchasing the jacket, you may inadvertently support the company's unethical practices through second- and third-order effects that result in someone being enslaved to produce it.

Next, let's examine investing in the S&P 500.

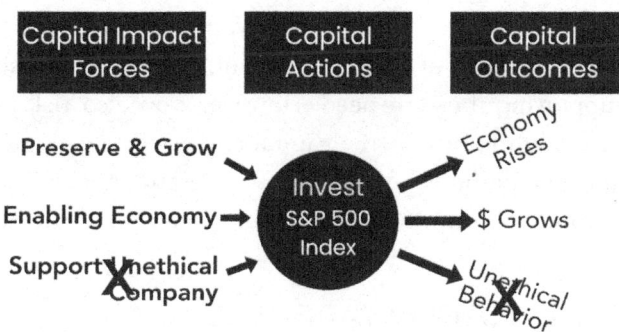

This is a straightforward capital investment action that most investors engage in. The outcomes typically include a rise in the economy, which tends to increase the value of your investment. From a Stewardship perspective, you are preserving and growing your wealth while also contributing to economic growth by adding value to these companies through your investments. However, if your investment supports an unethical company, this compromises the Alignment impact force by allowing that company to continue its harmful practices.

Some companies engage in unethical practices, such as developing atomic weapons or participating in human trafficking by employing individuals against their will. This issue became apparent to Tom Monaghan when he realized he was investing in companies that supported abortion rights, which gained traction after Roe v. Wade.

Another example is the act of donating all your money to charity.

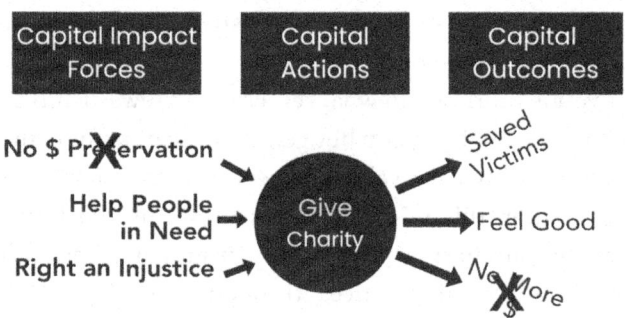

While this may seem virtuous on the surface, it can lead to unintended consequences. By giving away all your resources, you may help victims and feel a sense of accomplishment, thereby addressing injustices and supporting those in need. However, you also risk neglecting your responsibility to preserve the capital entrusted to you and growing it for your future and the benefit of future generations. This neglect may hinder your ability to continue your mission effectively in the future.

INCREASING YOUR AWARENESS

You may be asking, "How can I possibly know if there are negative effects on any of my Capital Actions?

It is a complex question, but it's the right one to ask at the right time. Here's a challenging example: how do you know whether the clothes you're wearing were manufactured or produced unethically, and what is your moral responsibility in that situation? This leads to the question discussed in chapter 7 about our degrees of culpability and responsibility.

We need to ask ourselves how far we want to take this issue. You will need to decide for yourself where the line is for you. The goal is not to scrutinize every single financial decision. The goal is to continue to move in the direction that supports your purpose through your mission.

It's not a simple matter, but the fact that you're asking that question shows that your mind is in the right place. The reality is that we don't want to think about these things.

For now, we'll focus on setting our list of Exclusions. By setting clear boundaries, you define your position, attract opportunities, and build relationships that align with your mission. This approach creates a framework for virtuous action while providing clarity, speed, and consistency in decision-making. It allows you to lead effectively and build a coalition to counteract the agenda of your Adversary.

Establishing Exclusions creates a playing field where you can initiate positive change, attract individuals to assist you, and pursue the common good. Now let's explore the other side of the Capital Impact Forces, focusing on the initiatives that can drive your mission forward without compromising ethics or morals.

CHAPTER 6
ELEVATIONS: OPPORTUNITIES TO ADVANCE YOUR MISSION

If our goal is to direct our capital toward genuine virtue in the pursuit of the good, the true, and the beautiful, then we should be willing to make sacrifices to pursue capital actions which advance them.

t's often difficult to pause and reflect on all the negative aspects we don't want to support, but it can be even more challenging to identify the positive things we do want to back. This isn't because there aren't good causes to support; rather, it's because there are so many worthwhile initiatives.

Narrowing down the specific efforts that align with our mission can feel almost impossible. We should not only aim to act in a moral and virtuous manner but also to pursue a greater good that exceeds what we could achieve on our own. A prime example of this is the Tim Tebow Foundation.

THE TIM TEBOW FOUNDATION'S MISSION TO ELEVATE

As we've discussed, the Tim Tebow Foundation has one of the clearest missions of any organization I've encountered. A significant strength of their mission lies in its exclusive focus on what they choose to support and the goals they aim to achieve. Tim and Demi-Leigh feel that they're wasting time if they're not pursuing this mission; their commitment to making a positive impact in the world is unwavering.

Growing up with missionary parents, Tim witnessed a great deal of suffering. He realized there was far more to life than merely living for oneself and those close to him; he understood he could contribute much more to the world.

As he transitioned into his role as a football player and public figure, Tim recognized the potential he had to further this mission. While there are many areas he wanted to commit support to, he knew that if he directed his efforts into focused areas, he could increase the impact he's able to have.

Tim thought about which communities were the most vulnerable and reflected on his childhood experiences. He became acutely aware of issues like human trafficking. Recognizing that some people were overlooked by society, he aspired to be a beacon of hope for those individuals.

Thus, he established a robust framework centered around four key areas. These priorities align with his values and address specific needs, despite the myriad of causes he could choose to support.

ELEVATIONS DEFINED

These priorities, which we will call "Elevations," are mission-aligned Capital Actions. Capital Actions are morally neutral in most cases. They, of course, must pass through your negative Exclusions Screen. However, Elevations are prioritized Capital Actions. They contribute to accelerating the mission's accomplishments, potentially requiring a rebalancing of the Capital Impact Forces.

Elevations are so mission-aligned that they are deemed to pursue a greater good. As a result, they often suggest a different prioritization for how you typically approach your mission through each of the Capital Impact Forces. For instance, you may need to compromise some of the goals and objectives that Stewardship would command to allocate more money toward something that may be heavy in purpose alignment but may not produce the returns or outcomes you would typically seek.

You may be asking, "So, are Elevations just like giving to feel good?"

Feel-good giving can be nice, and there's nothing wrong with it. However, is your mission simply to feel good? It's likely that your mission is to create a specific impact you want to see in the world.

Ideally, that impact will bring you a sense of satisfaction in the end, but it may not always feel that way during the process. In fact, the journey toward making an impact can, at times, be painful and difficult.

It's not about how you feel. What truly matters is that you are actively pursuing the impact you desire, in alignment with your purpose.

Elevations are prioritized because they are mission-accelerating and often require sacrifice.

YOUR ADVERSARY HATES OPPOSITION

Your Adversary can tolerate your exclusions. What they can't stand is your active opposition. They fear the moment you stop just avoiding harm and start actively building alternative systems.

So, what does your Adversary want? They want you to remain defensive rather than offensive. They prefer that you focus on avoiding bad things rather than building good things. They want your capital to be reactive, not proactive.

Their strategy is to overwhelm you with so many problems that you spend all your energy trying not to support harmful causes, leaving no resources for advancing positive ones. They want you to think that avoiding evil is the same as doing good.

What does your Adversary most fear you'll do? They fear that you'll move beyond defensive Exclusions to offensive Elevations. That you'll use your capital to build competing systems that make their harmful practices obsolete.

Elevations aren't just about feeling good. They're about strategic competition. When you fund mission-accelerating options, you don't just withdraw support from your Adversary. You actively defeat them.

THE FOUR PRINCIPAL ELEVATION CATEGORIES

When thinking about Elevations in relation to your purpose, the idea can feel daunting. There is so much good that can be done in the world. Where do you even begin?

Fortunately, there are time-tested models for categorizing these pursuits. As we've discussed, frameworks like ESG attempt to provide structure, but those categories, environmental, social and governance, are not truly fundamental. They are limited and more organizational than human.

By contrast, all Elevations can be understood through four principal categories that are deeply embedded in our shared human experience: the dignity of the human person, the common good, subsidiarity, and solidarity. They are woven into our very humanity. Across history, cultures and philosophies have recognized them as central to what it means to lift the human person.

The United Nations drew on these principles in its 1948 Universal Declaration of Human Rights and continues to reinforce them in its Sustainable Development Goals. The social humanism movement, which is grounded entirely in reason and compassion apart from theology, aligns with them as well. Organizations like the World Bank and the Gates Foundation also operate from similar assumptions. Even African cultural philosophy, namely ubuntu, reflects their essence. However, they may be most formally articulated in Catholic Social Teaching.

These four principles are not imported from outside of us. They are fundamental to human nature and universal to our condition. At the same time, they are always relative to context. Poverty in the U.S. looks very different from poverty in Calcutta, India. That's why applying them requires attentiveness both to our own circumstances and to the broader world we seek to elevate.

With that foundation, let's take a look at each of these individually.

HUMAN DIGNITY

Human dignity asserts that every person has inherent worth and should be treated with respect, regardless of age, status, ability, or contribution.

This matters because societies thrive when all individuals are protected, valued, and given an opportunity to live with dignity. Unlike plants or animals, every person inherently possesses a unique dignity.

In terms of capital investment, we should avoid financing enterprises that devalue or exploit people. Instead, we can prioritize investments that protect life, health, and individual rights.

Examples of upholding human dignity include pursuing ethical labor practices, providing companionship and a sense of purpose for seniors who may feel isolated, supporting individuals with disabilities, and engaging in anti-trafficking efforts. This principle is about recognizing the unique humanity and dignity of every individual.

COMMON GOOD

The second category, the common good, encompasses the shared conditions and systems that enable all members of society to thrive.

The common good allows all people to flourish collectively. We share this world and its resources, as well as each other. The saying "A rising tide lifts all boats" holds true when we embrace the welfare of everyone in society.

I often describe the common good as akin to a bird's-eye view, but even broader, it's more like a God's-eye view. If He were to observe everything happening at once, He would see how all the pieces fit together for the benefit of all people.

The significant implication of this is that it enables us to invest in infrastructure, housing, healthcare, and education, elements that facilitate communal cooperation. It also supports public goods and fosters social cohesion. Examples include affordable housing and broad access to clean water.

The common good can also be expressed through one's mission. This leads us to the concept of subsidiarity.

SUBSIDIARITY

Subsidiarity is one of the most overlooked and underappreciated principles. It asserts that challenges should be addressed at the most local and competent level, closest to those affected.

In the United States, this principle is foundational to our existence. People were weary of the authoritarian nature of a king and the monarchy they had come from. They desired a system that allowed local choice and voice in matters that directly impacted them.

Local solutions are often more effective, accountable, and empowering. When you are close to a situation, you understand the nuances that influence outcomes better than those who are further removed. Empowering those nearest to the information and the situation generally leads to better outcomes for the people most affected.

From a capital perspective, this means funding local initiatives, whether they are entrepreneurial ventures or community-led solutions. It involves supporting initiatives that empower those most directly impacted by these issues and avoiding over-centralized, top-down models that diminish individual agency.

This approach aims to support individual agency, allowing people to make decisions and choose what is right for them. Examples include community land trusts, microfinance programs that help individuals start their own businesses to support their families, and neighborhood revitalization efforts that provide communities with the resources they need to thrive.

SOLIDARITY

The fourth principle is solidarity, which emphasizes our interconnectedness. Our decisions should reflect concern for others, particularly the vulnerable or excluded.

Why does this matter? Societies that care for one another are more stable, resilient, and just. This reflects our shared humanity and inherent brotherhood and sisterhood.

From a capital perspective, solidarity prioritizes inclusive business models and supports social mobility, welcoming participation rather than excluding individuals. It gives preference to those who have previously been left out of opportunities by recognizing their humanity rather than judging them based on their circumstances.

Examples may include programs for refugee entrepreneurship that assist those displaced through no fault of their own, enabling them to regain their footing and contribute productively to society. Workforce development programs targeting underserved populations also exemplify this commitment.

ELEVATIONS AND THE CAPITAL IMPACT FORCES

Typically, Elevations are affiliated with Empowerment or Alignment. However, every elevation will likely disrupt the status quo you have established for the balance of the Capital Impact Forces.

Pursuing an elevation is like adjusting the controls on your aircraft to reach a higher altitude or a further destination. Each force must recalibrate to support the new mission priority. Let's take a look at how each force may be impacted.

Stewardship may find itself under a little elevation pressure. Typically, Stewardship holds the purse strings tightly, as it's focused on preservation and growth. But Elevations demand that Stewardship "give a little." It's a strategic adjustment to better accomplish your purpose.

Think about it this way. If your mission is to combat human trafficking and you discover a safe house that desperately needs funding, pure financial stewardship might say, "Wait for an opportunity to generate returns." However, mission-driven Stewardship recognizes that some opportunities can't wait for optimal financial conditions. The question becomes, "What's the highest and best use of this capital right now?" And in this case, the Empowerment force may carry more weight than Stewardship.

Empowerment is supercharged by Elevations. Elevations naturally align with Empowerment because they're designed to serve the greater good. But here's what's interesting. Elevations often require Empowerment to think bigger and longer term than typical charitable giving.

Remember, we're not just pursuing feel-good giving. We're pursuing transformational impact. Take the Tim Tebow Foundation's approach.

They're not just helping people with special needs. They're changing how entire communities view and include these individuals. That's Empowerment.

Alignment is the rudder in turbulent elevation pursuits. When you're pursuing Elevations, external pressure increases. People will question your choices. People want to know why your resources are being allocated to things that may make less sense to the rest of the world. It's Alignment that keeps you on course when the winds of criticism blow.

Many people make such choices. For example, consider someone facing significant medical expenses. If they believe their life is nearing its end, they may view their money as having much less value in the future than it does today. Consequently, they might decide to allocate all their resources toward a cause that preserves their life or enhances the lives of others.

On the other hand, pursuing elevated purposes will always require some level of reallocation within the Purpose-Driven Capital Framework. It becomes a question of where we will sacrifice some of our managed capital to favor Alignment or Empowerment, aiming to achieve specific outcomes through these elevated actions.

DISCERNING YOUR ELEVATIONS

How can we discern which of these four principles to pursue? Elevations are our capital priorities, and since they are prioritized, they often require a greater allocation of resources.

To facilitate this discernment process, there are three questions to consider:

1. What specific outcomes most directly align with your mission?
2. What areas are underserved by conventional capital?
3. What areas are you most uniquely prepared to respond to?

Let's dig deeper into each of these three questions and how to break them down further.

1. What specific outcomes align with your purpose?

We need to understand our purpose and recognize that certain principles and initiatives related to those four areas are aligned with the outcomes we are seeking. Identify the key elements of your mission and carefully discern what is important. To do this effectively, you must clearly understand your purpose. Consider which aspects of your mission are best positioned to serve your purpose.

With this in mind, it is easy to think about all the good that can be done. Think back to Tom Monaghan. He knew his core purpose, but he had lost his focus in the midst of success. In a sense, he experienced purpose drift, which refers to any activity that diverts attention away from your core purpose. It's like chasing a shiny object that's appealing but doesn't align with what you're supposed to be doing. This can be a significant drain on resources that better serve your mission.

To illustrate this, consider yourself a home builder. If you are skilled at constructing homes quickly and efficiently, that's a valuable, meaningful service. You may also know how to repair cars, but fixing one may take you days. Meanwhile, another mechanic can do the same job in an hour.

Even though you could fix the car, doing so would divert time, tools, and energy from your higher calling: building homes. The same is true for capital. When we direct it toward our unique purpose and mission, it can be like a superpower—working through us in ways that few, if any, could ever replicate.

2. What areas are underserved by conventional capital?

When we think about conventional capital, we refer to areas where significant funding is already available. For instance, the Tim Tebow Foundation recognized key areas where they are uniquely positioned to provide the greatest impact and have directed both the investment arm and foundation to focus on those. This strategy allows them to avoid becoming just another small contributor in well-supported areas and instead focus on those who truly need their support.

3. What areas are you uniquely prepared to respond to?

Everyone possesses unique gifts and resources. We need to identify where our purpose, underserved areas, and our unique capabilities intersect. This means determining where we can contribute the most value, especially in areas of high need. This approach helps us avoid the passive allocation of resources, where funds are distributed without careful consideration.

This concept relates to the idea of "blue ocean" versus "red ocean."[1] A "red ocean" signifies a market rife with competition, where many are vying for the same opportunities, akin to blood in the water. Nonprofits often face this challenge, competing to assist the same populations with similar needs.

In contrast, a "blue ocean" represents a space with less competition, allowing you to make a unique contribution. If you have the resources, capabilities, and mission to address a need in an area where few others are operating, that is where you may want to focus your efforts.

THE TWO MODES OF ELEVATIONS

Now we can begin to consider our actions. There are two primary modes through which Elevations can be enacted: social action and systemic change. Elevations have the most impact when these two modes are combined.

Social Action: This is often referred to as charity, which involves direct care or support for those in need. Examples of social action include feeding the hungry, supporting new mothers and families, providing disaster relief, and offering scholarships for students. In these cases, funds are directed straight to where the need exists, providing immediate relief.

Systemic Change: This mode is more strategic and involves advocacy, which focuses on influencing systems, culture, or laws. Examples include promoting ethical business practice, engaging with school boards, campaigning to end human trafficking, and advocating for the protection of vulnerable populations. In these scenarios, addressing the underlying issues often requires systemic change, rather than simply donating money.

Charity and advocacy work together to create progress toward any elevation you are pursuing. By integrating both approaches, you can effectively address immediate needs while also working toward lasting solutions.

Putting it all together, understanding your priorities and aligning them with effective actions, guides them toward more meaningful impact.

Elevations are most impactful when combined with social action and systemic change. To pursue Elevations to their fullest potential, we must first determine the good that can be done and then apply the four principles of social action—human dignity, the common good, subsidiarity, and solidarity—to discern which initiatives align most closely with our purpose. From there, we can identify underserved areas and our unique contributions. This process will help us create our list of Elevations.

ELEVATIONS FOR THE TIM TEBOW FOUNDATION

Once we have our list of Elevations, we will move into actions related to advocacy and charity to maximize our impact. Let's consider an example from the Tim Tebow Foundation, which provides a clear framework for discerning which initiatives to pursue based on three key questions:

1. What specific outcomes most directly align with their mission? Their answer is helping the most vulnerable people experience faith, hope, and love.
2. What areas are underserved by conventional funding? The foundation identified more heavily funded areas. While they still may contribute in these areas, their focus is on other areas where they are uniquely equipped to respond.
3. How could they use their brand and mission experience to rally public and political support for funding initiatives and advocacy? They use their brand credibility and mission results to create coordinated media campaigns to engage the

public and build political interest, even advocating to Congress to pursue support.

Based on this discernment, they chose four impact areas. Generally, Elevations are associated with Empowerment or Alignment but can influence all three impact forces. Pursuing these capital priorities has resulted in directly funding their mission, even admittedly at the expense of likely returns that could have resulted if not for pursuing these elevated priorities.

Let's look at a couple of examples.

EXAMPLE: FAITH-BASED VENTURE CAPITAL FUND

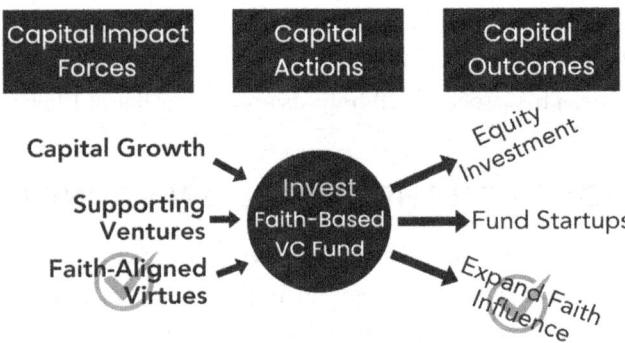

First, consider a faith-based venture capital fund. For someone like Tim Tebow or Tom Monaghan, who are pursuing faith-aligned values, investing in a faith-aligned venture fund might be an option. The Capital Outcome involves an equity investment that could yield greater returns in the future. Startups receive funding based on their value structures. From a Stewardship perspective, the capital growth comes from empowering ventures that align with their values. Notably, this investment allows them to expand their faith-aligned influence.

So what's the tradeoff? The capital may not grow as quickly as in a niche venture capital fund. This means there is a tradeoff in Stewardship, but by making this choice, they are better able to pursue a greater good.

EXAMPLE: TRAFFICKING SAFE HOUSE

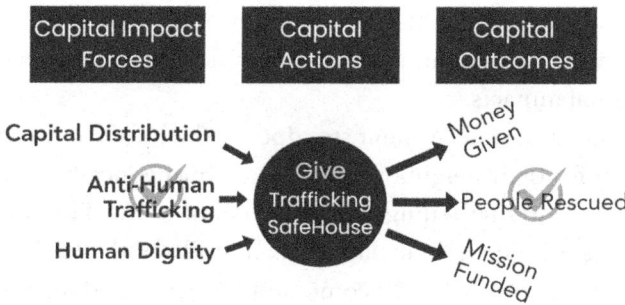

The second example involves funding a trafficking safe house. In this case, funds are directed to support their mission. From a Stewardship perspective, the capital is not being preserved. It is being allocated to a cause intended to uplift human dignity, but there is no expectation of that money being returned, let alone that there will be any additional financial returns as with an investment.

However, by focusing on anti-human trafficking efforts, they are directly helping individuals in need. This action elevates the impact of Empowerment and leads to successful outcomes, such as rescuing people from slavery. While there is a sacrifice in capital preservation, it is for the greater good of rescuing people.

EXAMPLE: LOCAL CONTRACTOR

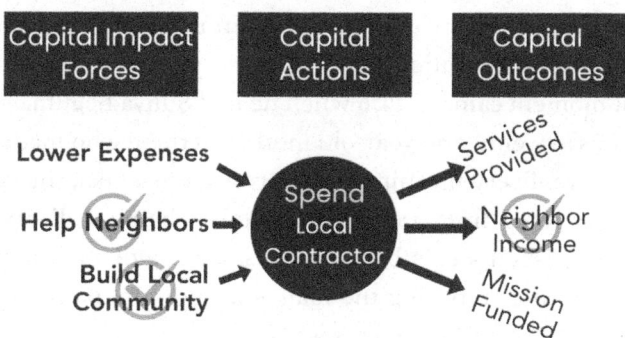

From a subsidiarity perspective, we can consider the impact of hiring locally versus hiring a lower-cost national contractor. When you choose to hire a local contractor, you not only receive the necessary services but also support the mission at hand. This decision potentially engages two positive capital impacts.

First, from an Empowerment standpoint, the local contractor creates employment for their neighbors. Second, by hiring locally, it aligns with the mission of strengthening the local community. This means that neighbors are benefiting financially, which fulfills both objectives.

While hiring locally might come at a higher cost than opting for a national contractor or lower brand recognition, this choice can be seen as a priority within particular mission focuses, as it redirects capital toward supporting the local community and the individuals who are employed as a result.

These actions represent a unique opportunity to intentionally use your capital to serve the world by enhancing human dignity, promoting the common good, and fostering subsidiarity and solidarity.

By carefully considering these steps, you can identify the right areas for your contributions to make a meaningful impact.

GRAMEEN BANK: SERVING A NEED, GROWING A BUSINESS, STARTING THE MICROFINANCE REVOLUTION

There are times when Elevations might seem to require a sacrifice but end up becoming a key driver of business. From a business standpoint, it turns into an elegant solution to a real-world problem. For Muhammad Yunus, that moment came in 1976 when he met Sufiya Begum.

Sufiya was a twenty-one-year-old mother of three who made bamboo stools to survive. Every morning, she borrowed five taka, the equivalent of about thirty cents, from a middleman to buy bamboo. Every evening, she sold her finished stools back to the same middleman for five taka and fifty paisa. After repaying the loan, she kept fifty paisa, the equivalent of about three cents, for a day's work.

When Yunus asked why she didn't buy her own bamboo, Sufiya looked at him like he didn't understand the world. "Where would I get twenty taka?" she asked. Twenty taka equals about one dollar and twenty-five cents. Yunus realized that was the barrier that stood between this hardworking woman and economic freedom.

She wasn't asking for charity or a handout. She was working, creating value. She just needed capital to work for herself.

Traditional banking would not work for people like Sufiya. Because of her poverty, she was viewed as a credit risk. She was too expensive to serve and too risky to trust. Lending to her violated their standards for Stewardship. However, the Empowerment impact force was largely ignored. Bankers at the time didn't care if it would help her build her life. They were reasonably but tragically focused on being responsible with their resources.

Yunus wondered if he could design a system where Empowerment could help strengthen Stewardship through a clear purpose... Alignment.

What he came up with was a system that revolutionized the banking industry. Instead of requiring collateral, he created group accountability. Five women would form a circle, and each member's success would depend on everyone else's success. Their social fabric became the collateral.

He decided to focus on women, as women statistically invest more of their earnings in family welfare, education, and community development.

Then he decided to measure success in a unique way. While he kept track of repayment rates, he also started to look at how many families moved out of poverty, how many children entered school, and how many women started businesses.

The results should have been impossible. Grameen Bank achieved a 97 percent repayment rate. That is better than most commercial banks' lending to wealthy clients. They reached over nine million borrowers, almost entirely women. They demonstrated that when structured properly, the poor could be among the most creditworthy borrowers in the world. Additionally, borrowers' children attended school at much higher rates, and these women gained decision-making power in their families. Entire villages transformed as microbusinesses flourished.

Sufiya's fifty-paisa profit became the spark that lit a global microfinance revolution. In 2006, the bank and Yunus received the Nobel Peace Prize for their work. Grameen became a global symbol of successful microfinance.

MOVING INTO PART III

Now that you know where you're going and have the basic tools to get there, we're going to get much more granular. I want to ensure you have a deep understanding of the implications of your spending, investing, and giving. I want you to feel confident that you know how to think through the process and each unique situation.

In Chapter 7, we're going to look at how to apply the tools you've built in real-world situations.

Then, in Chapter 8, we're going to look at how to evaluate your decisions in the future and continue to make better decisions.

Lastly, in Chapter 9, we'll review the process and discuss how to practically get started.

You've made it this far. I have no doubt that you're excited for the opportunity to put these concepts into practice. Let's make your purpose take flight!

PART THREE
BUILD YOUR PROCESS

CHAPTER 7
DECISION, DILIGENCE, AND DISCERNMENT

If our goal is to direct our capital toward genuine virtue in the pursuit of the good, the true, and the beautiful, we must look beneath the surface to evaluate the deeper effects of our actions while discerning which we will choose to take.

THE CHALLENGES OF MAKING FINANCIAL DECISIONS

In the reality of Capital Actions—spending, investing, and giving—there are always more opportunities than there are resources to act upon them. These opportunities may be presented in ways that do not accurately reflect their true impact. So, we must evaluate these opportunities to determine not only whether they are acceptable but also whether they are virtuous and worth pursuing.

This emphasizes the importance of due diligence. While due diligence is widely recognized in the investment world, as well as in philanthropy and even daily spending, its significance is heightened when viewed through the lens of purpose alignment. Due diligence helps us understand not only what we are spending, giving, and investing in but also the implications of these actions so we can anticipate their actual outcomes.

101

The three Capital Impact Forces—Stewardship, Empowerment, and Alignment—influence these outcomes, and we must develop our discernment process to make it second nature. The purpose of this chapter is to help you establish a framework to prepare mentally for any Capital Action decision. By doing so, we can approach these actions with clarity, knowing the desired outcomes and the pertinent questions to ask that will lead to those outcomes.

The central question, then, is how do you assess and discern the right Capital Actions to achieve your intended impact on the world?

CHAPTER ROAD MAP

I want to give you a heads up. This chapter is the most philosophical of all of them, so it may seem a bit dense. Consistent decision-making and discernment require structured thought. The strategies in this chapter will help you accomplish just that.

In this chapter, we will explore how to choose a particular Capital Action in a given situation by focusing on four key areas. First, we will revisit the purpose-aligned assessments discussed earlier, which provide the due diligence foundation you'll need. This process begins with evaluating the individual or organization.

Next, we will move on to the opportunity itself, focusing on exclusions, actions, or investments we should avoid. Third, we will consider potential enhancements or Elevations. Finally, we will delve into a deeper level of due diligence informed by the mission-aligned diligence we've discussed.

HOBBY LOBBY'S STAND

As a case study, let's take a look at Hobby Lobby's response to the 2010 Affordable Care Act. The Green family faced an ethical dilemma, leaving them with an existential question for their business and legacy. While centered around a deeply controversial and emotional topic, it is a strong illustration of principled action.

Hobby Lobby was at the center of a national debate surrounding a legislative movement regarding the Affordable Care Act, which mandated that most employers like Hobby Lobby include all FDA-approved contraceptives in their healthcare plans. Hobby Lobby, founded by David Green, has become one of the largest arts and crafts retailers in the United States, evolving into a multi-billion-dollar enterprise.

Initially, Green operated like a typical business owner, focusing on growth and operational efficiency. However, he identified as a Christian and generally ran his business according to Christian values. Despite this, he had not always been intentional about how deeply his faith influenced his decisions and day-to-day operations.

Eventually, Green began reflecting on how his supply chain investments might be indirectly supporting practices that conflicted with his Christian values. He also scrutinized how his business model mirrored his faith in terms of employee treatment and interactions. Additionally, he evaluated whether his philanthropic efforts were more transactional than transformational, especially given the significant resources and influence he had accumulated. While he didn't state it in quite this way, he determined that they were violations of his Exclusions. This prompted him to consider how he could best use his wealth and influence for positive change.

How could he lead his business to be transformational in addition to his personal transformation? The pivotal moment came with the passing of the Affordable Care Act and the subsequent scrutiny of its contraceptive mandate. David Green's company faced legal challenges because it refused to comply with this mandate, which required employers to provide coverage for contraceptives that Green believed caused abortions. As someone with strong Christian values, he was fundamentally opposed to any form of abortion and did not want to enable it. Consequently, he excluded such options from the healthcare plan.

This situation sparked a national conversation and became a focal point in the debate over religious freedom. It forced Green to critically evaluate how his financial resources were interconnected with moral decisions and whether he could remain passive. He had to consider the weight of his responsibility in managing and distributing that capital, especially when pressured by government mandates.

Hobby Lobby made significant efforts in this battle, eventually leading to a landmark Supreme Court case where the court ruled in the company's favor. This decision opened doors for many others to reevaluate how they operate their businesses. To achieve this, they needed to dive deeper into their social consciences, awakening this awareness in many people.

For Green and Hobby Lobby, the decision held special significance. They reorganized their business around a biblical framework, becoming more intentional in their practices. Though they had always closed on Sundays and aimed to treat their employees well, they implemented additional measures such as offering above-market wages and maintaining comprehensive health coverage consistent with their beliefs. They also restructured their estate plan to place company ownership into a trust, ensuring that it would remain a faith-based entity for future generations.

This example illustrates how deeply our capital can impact the world. Hobby Lobby not only aligned its mission with its owners' genuine religious convictions but also paved the way for others to do the same.

Hobby Lobby's decision to challenge this mandate and pursue legal action helped Green recognize his moral responsibility and the power they had to effect positive change in the world. This demonstrates the impact of financial decision-making. Whether you are making decisions for a multibillion-dollar corporation or for your own finances, the same principles can apply. Your decisions make an impact on how the world operates.

YOUR ADVERSARY WANTS TO SOW CONFUSION AND INDECISION

Your Adversary's most powerful weapon isn't opposition; it's confusion. They want you to get lost in analysis paralysis, overwhelmed by the complexity of making "perfect" decisions.

So what does your Adversary want? They want you to give up on values-based decision-making because it seems too complicated, time-consuming, or impossible to do perfectly. They want you to think that if you can't do it perfectly, why even start?

Their strategy is to flood you with contradictory information. They want to make ethical alternatives seem expensive and inconvenient and create so many moral gray areas that you retreat to your default choices... choices that may end up supporting their agenda.

So, what does your Adversary most fear you'll do? They fear that you'll develop a systematic decision-making process that handles complexity and helps you get past paralysis. That you'll pursue progress rather than only settling for perfection, and your consistent small improvements compound into significant change.

The purpose of your three assessments isn't to guarantee perfect outcomes. It's to ensure that your decisions consistently move in the right direction. Your Adversary needs you to be paralyzed by complexity. Your framework frees you to act.

YOUR THREE ASSESSMENTS

When it comes to making decisions, particularly those involving significant Capital Actions, the process doesn't have to be difficult. It doesn't require a years-long court battle to determine how you will allocate your financial resources. However, spending, investing, and giving your money does necessitate systematic thinking to ensure you achieve the desired Capital Outcomes from your actions.

In this book, we have established three assessments that can serve as a framework for making these decisions: the Purpose Assessment determines if there is mission fit, the Exclusions Screen identifies any immediate exclusions, and the Elevations Assessment evaluates whether the Capital Action will enhance your mission.

Nevertheless, these decisions are not always clear-cut. Let's examine each of these assessments individually and outline what the decision-making process may involve.

DECISION FATIGUE VS. PURPOSE SWITCH ACTIVATION

So, with all this in mind, why do smart, values-driven people make financial choices that contradict their stated beliefs? Decision fatigue disables the Purpose Switch. When every financial choice requires complex moral reasoning, your cognitive resources get depleted. You end up making decisions based on convenience rather than conscience.

The three assessments, Purpose, Exclusions, and Elevations, are designed to prevent this cognitive overload. By doing the heavy moral reasoning upfront when creating your screens, you preserve mental energy for implementation. Your Purpose Switch can function properly because you're not re-litigating fundamental values with every decision.

You can think of it this way. A clear Exclusions list means you don't have to debate whether to invest in tobacco companies every time you see a fund that includes them if you've already eliminated them. The decision is pre-made, cognitive load is reduced, and your Purpose Switch can focus on identifying positive opportunities rather than getting bogged down in avoiding negatives.

CONDUCTING YOUR PURPOSE ASSESSMENT

For the Purpose Assessment, you need to consider three questions before proceeding:

- Does this action align with our financial strategy?
- Does it uplift those involved?
- Is it consistent with our values?

While these questions seem straightforward, they require deeper exploration. This deeper dive occurs when you have thoroughly shaped your conscience and understand the various Capital Impact Forces at play. Each question corresponds with one of these Capital Impact Forces, guiding you to think critically about them even before you assess whether the Capital Action passes your negative screen or benefits from your Elevations Assessment.

This process involves two phases: examining the actor and the action. The actor performs the Capital Action. Remember, you get to choose *who* you collaborate with to accomplish your mission.

ASSESSING THE ACTOR

The actor is serving your mission on your behalf using your capital. They drive three key aspects: how the action is formulated (what will take place), how the action is executed (the methodology of the action), and how the action presents externally (the reputational stakes, affiliations, and standards at play).

There are three factors to consider when assessing an actor:

1. **External Actions:** What do they do and stand for publicly? How are they perceived?
2. **Internal Operations:** How do they behave internally? Their mission, culture, integrity.
3. **Extraordinary Actions:** What affiliations or partnerships extend beyond their core work? Do these align with your core values?

Imagine an investment fund manager. We will want to look first at their external actions. The fund manager is marketing themselves as an impact fund seeking to enhance economic opportunity in poverty-stricken areas of Africa. We can see how they present themselves on their website and their public personas. What are their mission, vision, and values? Do any of these things contradict? Are they engaging in activities that obviously contradict those?

When evaluating their internal operations, you can compare their mission and values and see whether those are actively exhibited. Does their financial distribution support that? Are they properly representing their stakeholders?

This process doesn't have to be complex, but it should be intentional. Develop a simple mental framework—even a checklist at first—to ask: Do their actions, operations, and affiliations align with the good we seek to advance?

You may want to formalize this with a checklist of things to look for at first, but the point here is alignment. You are looking for people who are not only performing work aligned with your mission but who will effectively and consistently represent your mission well.

Now let's move into assessing the actions themselves, starting with your Exclusions Screen.

DISCERNING EXCLUSIONS

You should now have a clear idea of your Exclusions, but the question remains: At what point is each exclusion triggered?

To some degree, we are all complicit in various activities in the world. For instance, taxes in the United States support a wide range of activities, prompting us to consider our level of complicity in these actions. How much ignorance is acceptable regarding issues we should be aware of?

Once you establish your Exclusions, you should be able to recognize them quickly and easily. However, determining your culpability for these exclusions can be challenging.

HOW CLOSE IS TOO CLOSE: ORDERS OF PROXIMITY

To understand your level of culpability, consider how closely connected you are to a particular ethical or moral violation. This brings up the question of how close is too close, or sometimes, how far is too far, especially under the assumption that you do not intend to support any moral violations.

This analysis can be rooted in Thomistic moral theology. St. Thomas Aquinas developed a framework to help people understand their proximity to sin, and over the years, it has been formalized to broadly assess ethical situations. Moral theologians and ethicists have used this framework to describe situations and discern whether something is morally acceptable or not.

Aquinas identified four orders of proximity that are now commonly recognized: formal cooperation, immediate material cooperation, mediate material cooperation, and remote material cooperation. Each degree indicates varying levels of proximity to the immoral act.

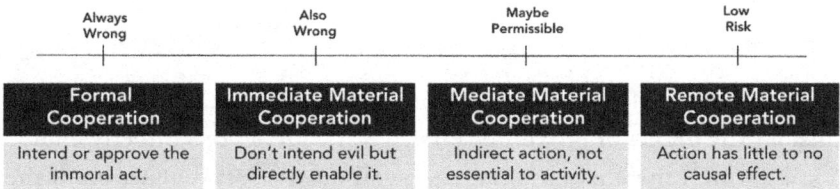

The closest proximity is formal cooperation, which occurs when you support or approve of an immoral act. If your exclusion involves something you oppose morally and you actively engage in or approve of that action, you are in formal cooperation with it.

The second degree, immediate material cooperation, occurs when you do not intend to engage in an immoral act, but you directly enable it. For example, if you know an organization acts unethically and, rather than distancing yourself or withdrawing support, you continue to buy from them or provide funding, you are participating in immediate material cooperation with their actions.

The next degree of moral proximity is immediate material cooperation, which involves indirect action. Although this form of cooperation is not essential to the activity, you are still providing some level of support.

For example, consider an organization engaged in an activity that contradicts your moral principles. You are not directly supporting or purchasing from them, but you may be facilitating their existence. Imagine that people are directed to this organization through a channel you control. If you leave that channel open, you are allowing individuals who are being wronged to access a source of moral harm. While you are not directly participating in the wrong, you are indirectly enabling its existence.

The fourth degree of proximity is remote material cooperation. Here, your action has little to no causal effect. As members of humanity, we are intrinsically connected, but remote material cooperation implies that, as a mere member of this network, you are not actively cooperating, directly, indirectly, or otherwise, with the negative activity you are trying to avoid. Your mere existence has little impact on that harmful action.

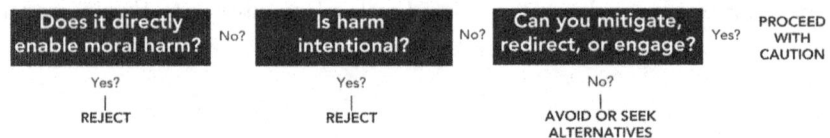

To determine if you are too close to a morally questionable situation, consider the orders of proximity. First, ask if your actions directly enable moral harm. If the answer is yes, then you must reject that action. If the answer is no, consider whether the harm is unintended or indirect. If the harm is unintended or indirect, you then need to assess whether you can mitigate, redirect, or engage with this specific action to prevent your moral culpability. If you find that you cannot, you should avoid that action or seek alternatives. If you can mitigate, redirect, or engage, then you may proceed with caution.

MITIGATE, ENGAGE, REDIRECT

Morally ambiguous actions can sometimes be permissible, or even encouraged, provided there is a proper strategic intent behind them. If your actions might unintentionally cause harm, you can still proceed by employing one of three approaches: mitigation, redirection, or engagement.

MITIGATE

To avoid moral culpability in situations where harm may or may not occur, mitigation is often the best option. Mitigation involves reducing the degree or likelihood of harm within the existing action or relationship without altering its structure. This method usually requires conditional participation, where you implement moral safeguards in your agreement or involvement in the particular financial arrangement.

For example, suppose you are involved with an agriculture company that sources cocoa. This is generally a positive activity, as it supports farmers and provides food. However, you are aware that suppliers in this industry have a problematic history of child labor. To mitigate this risk, you could require the fund or entity you are investing in to adopt strict supplier audits, transparency reports, and third-party certifications. These measures would allow your investment to proceed without the risk of unintentionally supporting morally questionable practices.

REDIRECT

Redirection is where you require the organization to cease or remove the unethical component as a condition of your support. This proactive approach ensures that the organization changes its practices. You maintain your intent but alter your approach.

For instance, consider an investment in a venture capital firm that funds biomedical startups. You know that this firm is open to investing in embryonic stem cell research, but your mission and organization do not consider this research morally acceptable and have excluded such investments from your portfolio.

To address this, you can redirect the firm by requiring it to remove the option of investing in startups engaged in embryonic stem cell research from its investment strategy.

ENGAGE

The third approach is engagement, where the situation can become morally complex. This involves directly participating in an activity that you believe to be morally wrong with the purpose of being a voice to promote morally good action. Here, you maintain your investment or relationship with the express intention of influencing positive change. This is a form of internal advocacy.

You must approach this with the goal of driving change. If your intent is merely to stay involved for personal gain or be a positive presence, that is not the objective of the engagement strategy. The main purpose is to facilitate change in that particular organization.

We often see this in public companies, where shareholder advocates pursue change. For example, consider a public technology company that produces goods under poor labor practices overseas. If you engage with this company as a shareholder, you do so with the knowledge of these practices, while most shareholders are content with the profits generated and tend to ignore these moral issues.

By becoming involved, you can advocate for better labor practices, and there are many instances where public companies have changed their practices due to internal advocacy from engaged shareholders.

One example of this happened in 2022: JPMorgan Chase was facing sharp criticism when its subsidiary, WePay, was enforcing a "social risk" policy that barred doing business with certain clients based on subjective criteria. This impacted faith-based and conservative organizations, which had been de-banked under this policy, cutting them off from services.

The policies in place allowed people to make subjective decisions because their views were unpopular with the decision-makers. It was a clear case where a corporation allowed ideological bias to determine who could be its customers.

Rather than divest, a group of shareholders filed a resolution demanding that JPMorgan address the problem directly. They pressed management to explain how it would ensure viewpoint neutrality in serving customers and remove the problematic policies. The resolution went to a proxy ballot where the investors could make the decision.

This forced JP Morgan's hand. They dropped the "social risk" restrictions from WePay and publicly affirmed that it would serve clients regardless of political, social, or religious affiliation. Because this was done before the vote, the resolution was withdrawn. The shareholders had successfully engaged with the company and won a victory benefiting folks from all different ideological convictions, preventing them from future discrimination.

So, these are the three methods—mitigation, redirection, and engagement—that you can use when navigating morally gray situations to create a positive outcome for yourself and others involved. According to this framework, culpability decreases with ignorance or coercion, although it may not be entirely eliminated.

DISCERNING CULPABILITY IN EXCLUSIONS

As members of the human race, we are all connected in various ways and may, in part, participate in immoral or negative actions. Even if you accept some ignorance of these actions, pursuing this framework can make it possible for your organization, or you personally, to have minimal moral culpability.

It is up to you to determine your level of culpability and the risks you're willing to take when engaging in financial actions. The critical question to ask is whether a potential violation is a non-negotiable issue.

Proximity matters, so how likely is the violation to happen? Can you mitigate, redirect, or engage in a way to reduce the risk?

If there's no option to lessen your culpability, then you need to decline. But what about situations where the answer is "maybe"? You may come across questions where your response is, "I simply don't know."

The situation might work out fine, but you could still be unsure about how to proceed. Are you willing to accept the risk of moving forward?

First, we need to recognize that ambiguity is inevitable. You can't know everything. Often, especially when considering Capital Actions through the Purpose-Driven Capital Framework, we understand that our decisions have long-term outcomes that extend far beyond the initial action. These short-term capital decisions almost always lead to long-term implications.

But can we claim "ignorance" as a valid option to reduce our culpability? Being ignorant can be a valid reason, but it is not always an excuse. We all have areas where we lack knowledge; in fact, we are ignorant of most things. It's impossible for us to know everything about ourselves, let alone the entire universe, right?

Therefore, a degree of ignorance is inevitable. The question of accountability arises when we consider what we should know and what we ought to pursue. Are we actively choosing not to seek out that knowledge? If we decide not to pursue something we should be aware of, even if we don't realize it, we remain ignorant. We often don't even know what we don't know.

For instance, I spoke with a successful person who is a strong Christian. During our conversation, we touched on human cloning. He shared his perspective. He couldn't understand why people, including his church, were concerned about it. He saw it differently and stated quite plainly that he didn't see the problem and didn't care to learn more.

He recognized that his church, among many others, opposes human cloning for ethical reasons, but he chose to remain uninformed rather than seek to understand the differing viewpoint and therefore the potential moral incongruence with his actions. One can understand a perspective and still disagree with it, which is perfectly acceptable. However, to deliberately choose not to understand an issue simply to avoid engaging with it is to *choose* to be ignorant. Within this context, that choice likely carries moral culpability. Whether large or small, there are lasting consequences. It's worth taking the time to understand the risks, clarify our moral distance, and determine whether we can participate "in good conscience."

FORMING YOUR MISSION CONSCIENCE

The final question to ask is, How much risk am I willing to take regarding my culpability and my organization's culpability in this action? This boils down to forming what I call your "mission conscience." Moral matters are inherently complicated, which highlights the importance of understanding your mission and taking the time to develop your mission conscience.

Your mission conscience serves as the decision maker regarding all your moral culpability questions. This process doesn't happen quickly; it requires wisdom and time to form. Your mission conscience represents the collective ability to make decisions based on the Capital Impact Forces, using the lenses you've established, and determining how deeply to engage in those lenses as you continue making Capital Actions.

Now let's explore Elevations. Your mission conscience should not only inform you about what to avoid but also illuminate when and where you should take action.

DISCERNING ELEVATIONS: LEARNING FROM THE OVERDECK FOUNDATION

In order to give your mission the boost it needs to take flight, you must do something more than simply avoid harm. It is about elevating those areas that move your mission forward. But how do you discern which initiatives to pursue?

Laura and John Overdeck give us a great example in practice. They began with a simple belief: Every child deserves the chance to discover their potential. From that mission, they built a disciplined process for making their Elevation decisions. Their foundation directs resources into five priorities: Early Impact, Exceptional Educators, Innovative Schools, Inspired Minds, and Data for Action.

What makes their model powerful isn't just what they fund, but how they decide. Every opportunity is weighed by strict criteria:

- Does it fit one of the five priorities?
- Can it produce measurable, lasting impact?
- Is the organization ready to sustain and scale?
- Will it influence the field, not just a single program?

Even research must be preregistered, with the results being published openly whether flattering or not. This transparency protects their mission and ensures their capital elevates what really works.

The outcomes are tangible. Math programs reach millions of students, and tools like GreatSchools are helping parents make better choices. The Overdeck Foundation reminds us that Elevations become real when guided by process.

That same principle can work for you as you develop your discernment process. Elevations show up in spending, investing, and giving. In spending, ask, "Are there products or providers that align with our mission or have the potential to advance a greater good?" In investing, consider how your capital can both generate returns and serve your mission. In giving, direct funds to the organizations and initiatives that best elevate your purpose.

The process is the same whether you manage a household budget or an institutional portfolio. Like the Overdecks, having a process for discerning your Elevation Capital Actions will help you guide Capital Outcomes that are more consistently aligned with your mission and have a longer-lasting impact.

IMPACT INVESTING FOR YOUR MISSION

Regarding spending and giving, the distinctions are generally clear. With spending, you understand what you receive, and typically, you are aware of the capital actors behind your support. Giving is, in many ways, similar.

You generally understand the mission you are supporting and can identify the key stakeholders involved, including their staff, teams, and boards of directors.

However, investing differs in significant ways. In recent years, there has been a rapid development of social consciousness. People have been contemplating impact investing under various names and forms and are increasingly considering where their money is going and what it supports.

For most people, investing has become passive and isn't a primary focus, unlike spending or giving. Therefore, I want to specifically examine the concept of impact investments. In recent years, this term has been defined more narrowly by organizations seeking to establish its purpose.

The Global Impact Investing Network (GIIN) defines impact investments as those "made with the intention of generating positive, measurable social or environmental impacts alongside a financial return."[1] While this is certainly commendable and something many can and do support, it is limited. It aligns with a specific mission, but not necessarily yours.

When considering impact investment, think about both its global definition and the concept of subsidiarity, which emphasizes addressing issues at the most local level, meaning your mission and that of your organization.

The Purpose-Driven Capital Framework offers a different definition, one related to your mission and organization. Here, capital is described as actions directed toward a strategic priority that intentionally advances the individual or organization's mission. This framework centers on individual missions rather than external definitions of impact.

When various organizations worldwide define what impact means, they may not consider your unique gifts and contributions. You are empowered to think about impact investing in terms of your mission rather than theirs.

Now, how do you measure impact? While we will delve deeper into this in the next chapter, we need to recognize the variations and categories of measurement. Not all actions or activities produce the same effect. Impact can be assessed from different perspectives, such as financial versus mission-driven outcomes, reflecting the tension between capital and impact.

DEGREES OF IMPACT

We will begin by exploring the degrees of impact. Impact is determined not only by actions taken but also by the extent of their effect. For example, $100 will typically have less impact than a million dollars for almost any organization or individual. However, this is based on monetary value, not necessarily on social or emotional significance; in some contexts, $100 could have a more profound impact than a million.

In general, more capital does achieve greater outcomes than less. For instance, covering someone's college costs may have less impact than creating a scholarship fund, and that fund may have less impact than endowing a scholarship that continues indefinitely. Likewise, purchasing fair trade certified coffee is commendable, but it may have less impact than investing in a regenerative agriculture fund, which could be even less impactful than funding legislative changes that shape agricultural practices globally for the long term.

It is clear that not all impact is equal. Different actions have different degrees of effect. This needs to be taken into consideration with your Capital Actions. Next, we will consider the priority of that impact.

PRIORITY OF IMPACT

The impact of various Capital Actions can vary significantly, leading us to prioritize certain initiatives over others. This prioritization often differs from one type of Capital Action to another, resulting in some actions receiving lower priority and others ranking higher.

For example, the transition to renewable energy is commendable, as it helps make energy sources more reliable and accessible worldwide. However, this may be viewed as a lower priority compared to access to mental health care, which is invaluable for people seeking support for their mental health needs. An even higher priority than mental health access is ensuring that people have access to food, as survival takes precedence over all other concerns. This hierarchy of priorities is not absolute and can differ among individuals.

THE TIM TEBOW FOUNDATION MODEL

The Tim Tebow Foundation has developed a compelling model for assessing the impact of various Capital Actions, using a matrix with an X and Y axis and four quadrants. The X axis represents profit potential, while the Y axis reflects mission focus. As we move up the Y axis, mission focus increases, and as we move right along the X axis, profit potential increases.

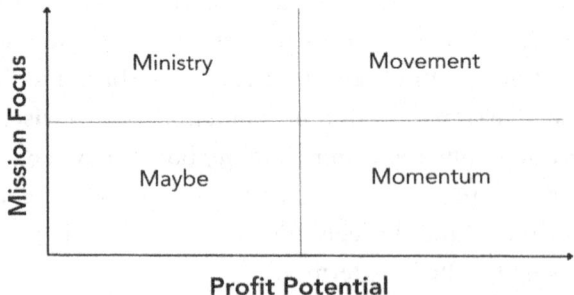

The upper-right quadrant represents the ideal scenario, where both mission focus and profit potential align. However, as the Tim Tebow Foundation points out, companies or organizations can change positions within this matrix over time.

The lower-left quadrant is labeled "Maybe," indicating potential opportunities that are not yet guaranteed. The upper-left quadrant is termed "Ministry"; these are opportunities worth funding because they benefit the mission, even if they may not generate profit. The lower-right quadrant represents "Momentum," which signifies progress towards mission goals without direct alignment to the mission. Finally, the upper-right quadrant is called "Movement," where there is full alignment with both mission and profit.

The Tim Tebow Foundation emphasizes that while the "Maybe" quadrant may appear less appealing for capital investment, injecting capital into these opportunities can transform them into "Ministries," then into "Momentum," and eventually elevate them to the "Movement" quadrant. This model effectively illustrates the dual focus on mission and profit that organizations can pursue.

Two approaches can facilitate progress in these initiatives: charity and advocacy. For meaningful progress, both elements must work together.

INCORPORATING THE TWO MODES: CHARITY AND ADVOCACY

As you evaluate your Capital Actions, consider whether they align with charitable causes, providing direct care or support to those in need (the charity foot), and whether they also involve advocacy, influencing systems, culture, and laws to create a sustainable framework (the advocacy foot).

When one of these two "feet" moves forward, it enables the other to do so as well. That is how your mission makes real progress toward your purpose. This is when direct actions become increasingly backed by the systemic structure that supports them.

The Tim Tebow Foundation, for instance, not only provides financial support to anti-human trafficking organizations, but it also backs businesses that contribute to these organizations. Additionally, the foundation works on legislative initiatives to establish a supportive framework for these efforts. This approach allows the foundation to address the direct causes of human trafficking, support those who enable solutions, and create a safety net for individuals who might fall through the cracks to help those in greatest need.

This comprehensive strategy requires thorough due diligence, which is necessary for any capital initiative. The Purpose-Driven Capital Framework will naturally guide you toward that deeper due diligence, preparing you for future decisions. Initially, it allows you to analyze the outward implications of the businesses you consider.

Internally, you can explore these businesses' intent, actions, and external impacts. Moreover, you should examine the unique characteristics of the capital actors involved, diving beyond the surface to understand their deeper connections and broader implications that may affect your mission.

THE MODEL'S CHALLENGE

This process is not easy and requires time and careful thought. Forming a clear mission conscience is a critical step. Once established, this conscience makes doing due diligence more intuitive.

Through Exclusions, you assess the level of risk you are willing to accept and the measures you will take to mitigate it, thereby reducing your potential liability. With Elevations, you evaluate how much positive impact you aim to achieve and how much capital you are prepared to invest to reach that goal.

It is invaluable to develop a systematic approach to consistently pursue your mission. The last thing you want is for your Adversary to exploit any weaknesses in your strategy, which could occur if you fail to implement a thorough process and system.

But never forget: it is *your* capital. You can walk away from any decision that doesn't align with your purpose. You can demand transparency from any organization asking for your support. You can choose to fund only what advances your values.

Your Adversary wants you to feel trapped by complexity, overwhelmed by imperfect options, and paralyzed by moral gray areas. But you're not trapped. You have more power than you realize, and now you have the tools to use it.

The framework doesn't guarantee perfect decisions. It helps our decisions consistently move in the right direction. Do this enough, and the world around you will start moving toward your mission.

CHAPTER 8
ONGOING ASSESSMENT —MONITORING YOUR OUTCOMES

If our goal is to direct our capital toward genuine virtue in the pursuit
of the good, the true, and the beautiful, we must ensure that the outcomes
we assessed when choosing our Capital Actions are still
the ones we are seeing after making that commitment.

Alright, you've discerned a Capital Action that aligns with your mission and purpose! Now what?

The outcomes of your Capital Actions can and most often do extend well beyond the initial commitment. While some actions may have a short-lived impact and require less commitment, others can create lasting effects on both us and the world, requiring a more significant investment of time and effort.

WHAT'S MEASURED GETS MANAGED

Because circumstances change over time, you must continuously monitor the outcomes to ensure that they align with your intended goals. This can be challenging, but it becomes second nature once you've established what you want to measure. By doing so, you can effectively manage those metrics.

It's important to keep an eye on what really matters when it comes to your spending, investing, and giving, but it doesn't have to dominate your life or your thoughts. You will come to intuitively know this framework once you set it up.

However, it's more than just defining your mission. It's putting something behind it so you can see your progress. It's good to feel positive about your investing and giving, but you have to ask yourself, *Am I truly creating the outcomes that I intended?* Without the right metrics, ones that you can reasonably manage, you may never know.

So, when can metrics go wrong? Well, to show this, let's take a look at a fictional nonprofit, which we'll call "The Common Good Project." While not a real example, it's a real situation that's happened in many nonprofits.

RIGHT HEART, WRONG METRICS: A CASE STUDY

The Common Good Project was placed in a low-income community where families were clearly struggling below the poverty line, and one of the most basic needs that this nonprofit wanted to solve was hunger. It was noticed that families were experiencing all kinds of problems due to a lack of nutrition: kids weren't performing in schools, adults were unable to provide for their families, and food had become a primary focus.

The nonprofit understood that if it took food off these families' list of worries, they could help free them to accomplish more with their lives. So, they set out to create a food distribution ministry. Of course, the main metric they tracked was pounds of food distributed to numbers of families, and they were very proud of the work they were doing. They saw that the numbers continued to increase as they grew their ministry over time.

The Common Good Project realized that this low-income area clearly needed help, and as they established more systems to engage more of the community, the numbers kept rising. They were helping more people, and new faces were coming in. They even noticed other nonprofits coming into the community to help because of their efforts to bring more attention to the plight of the folks there, and these other nonprofits started offering similar services.

Eventually, at a board meeting, a member respectfully pointed out, "We're doing great work, and we're offering food to people who genuinely need it, but why are we here? Are these families being freed from their poverty? Are fewer people actually hungry as a result of our efforts?"

So, The Common Good Project took a deeper look. They soon discovered that the faces they were seeing were the same as when they'd started their programs. They also realized that there were people there who didn't seem to have the same level of need as those they had origi-nally intended to serve.

Had they missed the mark? After a period of personal reflection, they determined that they needed to reevaluate the outcomes of all their programs, not just the food program. They needed to establish new systems that would actually lead to their end mission. So, they devised new metrics to help assess the needs of those coming into the line to determine whether food was a need that would help them become self-sufficient.

The Common Good Project began to track not only who was coming in, but how their lives were changing as a result. Because of the data they were receiving, they were able to pivot, shifting their resources and providing new services like job training, housing, and life skills. Instead of just feeding people, they began to truly free them from the burdens they were experiencing that the nonprofit might not have otherwise known had they not tracked these metrics.

The new programs complemented the programs offered by other local nonprofits, and over time, the community improved. The Common Good Project began to see the results of their offer. They saw their mission being fulfilled.

Though they'd had outstanding numbers from the beginning, they'd been tracking the wrong metrics. It was only when they evaluated the true outcomes, when they were able to change their metrics to deter-mine a path to success, a path toward their mission, that they had the impact that they had originally set out to make.

We want to do the same for you so that your Capital Actions serve the outcomes you want to see.

YOUR ADVERSARY IS OPPORTUNISTIC

Your Adversary knows that good intentions without ongoing accountability lead to purpose drift. They're patient. They'll wait for you to become busy, distracted, or overconfident before they exploit the gaps in your system.

So, what does your Adversary want? They want you to set up your values-based systems once and then assume they'll run on autopilot. They want you to trust without verifying, hope without measuring, and commit without monitoring.

Their strategy is to wait for your life to get too busy, for your focus to shift to new opportunities, and for your enthusiasm to fade. They know that organizations and people drift toward compromise when no one is watching the metrics that matter.

So, what does your Adversary most fear you'll do? They fear that you'll build accountability systems that catch drift before it becomes betrayal. They don't want you to look beyond vanity metrics and measure what matters to your mission.

Your Adversary counts on your assumption that good people automatically do good work. Your monitoring system transforms good intentions into measurable impact over time. When you track what truly matters, drift becomes visible and decisions become simpler.

YOUR MONEY, YOUR POWER, YOUR RESPONSIBILITY

If your capital offers you the opportunity to impact other people's decisions and lives, then capital is giving you a type of power—and with any power comes responsibility. You must ensure that your resources are not funding your Exclusions or supporting your Adversary's cause, either upfront or on an ongoing basis. We have already covered the upfront considerations; now we will focus on what ongoing assessment entails.

If we aim to measure what truly matters, we need to understand the common saying "What gets measured gets managed." Therefore, you must create a Capital Action management system, which consists of three components:

1. Start with the end in mind: Identify your key metrics.
2. Determine data sources: Establish your actual metrics and decide how frequently you want to assess them.
3. Create a system: Evaluate the data according to the established system.

Let's explore each of these components, beginning with the end in mind.

START WITH THE END IN MIND

Steven Covey's *7 Habits of Highly Successful People* offers tremendous insight with Habit 2: Start With the End in Mind. Consider the outcomes you are seeking. Mentally or in writing, reverse-engineer those outcomes to identify the causes that led to their occurrence.

You will develop a process that can visualize or outline the steps necessary to achieve those outcomes. Based on this understanding, you can set expectations for what you should see along the way as you progress toward them. Starting with the end in mind helps you establish a process that creates a series of signposts or metrics to properly assess whether the desired outcomes will materialize.

DATA SOURCES AND FREQUENCY

To determine your key metrics, start by identifying what will truly advance your mission. While your competitors may focus on vanity metrics, you should prioritize mission metrics.

What are vanity metrics? These are numbers that demonstrate activity but don't reflect actual results. This can include social media likes and press mentions. While they provide a sense of activity, they do not demonstrate real alignment with mission objectives. ESG ratings can also fall into this category, as they often only reflect how actions conform to predetermined criteria without illustrating the tangible outcomes achieved.

Conversely, mission metrics tell a compelling story about progress toward your mission. For example, you might measure the percentage of funds directed toward mission-impact initiatives or track the metric tons of carbon actually removed in an ESG context. In the nonprofit example mentioned earlier, instead of focusing on the total weight of food distributed, they could measure the percentage of people who achieve self-sufficiency.

When establishing your key metrics, focus on outcomes that directly relate to your mission, rather than on activities. Then consider your data sources and how frequently you'll assess them. Data can come from various channels, such as reports, newsletters, or direct communications with your team. Determine how often you will receive this data, whether daily, monthly, quarterly, or annually, based on the availability and distribution schedule of these sources, as well as your own information-gathering initiatives.

DATA EVALUATION SYSTEM

This effort should culminate in a simple and efficient data evaluation system. Tracking your data should not be time-consuming. When you understand your metrics and desired outcomes, it should be straightforward to assess whether your data supports your goals or not.

The first step is to clarify what you're seeking. Make sure you understand what your metrics represent and whether they are trending positively or negatively. Next, apply critical thinking skills to analyze the data. For example, if you notice that more meals are being distributed by the nonprofit, ask whether this increase is genuinely helping people or simply enabling them to continue harmful habits.

Lastly, keep a simple record of your findings to identify trends and predict future outcomes. A spreadsheet or even a notebook can serve as an effective tool for tracking this information.

You can use any format as long as it consolidates all your data in one location, as this helps you avoid having to remember everything. This approach allows you to visually track elements of progress, change, or even the static nature of certain aspects. Consequently, it becomes easier for you to assess the situation yourself.

MEASURING IMPACT

If I had to pick one lesson that nonprofits could give the financial world, it would be how to measure impact. Nonprofits thrive by securing supporters' buy-in to their mission. Their supporters are not measuring success by the profit they are bringing in. They are measuring it on the IMPACT they have according to their mission!

I experienced this firsthand as a professional nonprofit fundraiser. If you've ever given to a nonprofit, I guarantee you can relate to this experience. When we were seeking more donor support, we loved to share data. We shared data on the amount of financial assistance, food distributed, and hours of counseling provided. While the numbers were impressive, they didn't provide context. Client stories, however, were absolute gold, and I loved offering stories.

Stories share the human experience of impact, and we had some great ones. When I would tell people about the Wilsons, who lost everything in the 2016 Memorial Day floods, which struck the Greater Houston area, people understood that sense of loss. Donors could, in a sense, relate to the challenges and pain they experienced. But then to tell them that it was because of their financial support that we were able to pull together the community's resources to help the Wilsons get a temporary place to stay, clothes to wear, food to eat, new work tools to generate income, their home repaired, and new furniture, all at a fraction of the time and money they would have had to expend if on their own—that was powerful.

The most powerful piece, however, was not the resources we were able to provide the Wilsons. It was the reality that this family went from experiencing life on the border of poverty to total material loss, then back to self-sufficiency. The story demonstrated the true impact on their lives: they were once again contributing members of society, living in dignity.

But then we had to measure that, and we did. We shared these stories to bring the numbers to life. Because of that, we were able to numerically demonstrate that the amount of financial assistance and case management resulted in a number of families who were able to achieve self-sufficiency.

THE PROBLEM WITH IMPACT INVESTING METRICS

When it comes to impact investing, very few have this mindset. In my humble experience, this is because they are still viewing the activity as an "investing" activity rather than an "impact" activity, even if the investment is generating minimal returns.

There have been many attempts at this. B Corps are one example. A "Certified B Corporation" is a private certification offered by a nonprofit, B Lab. They have successfully lobbied multiple state governments to adopt the "Benefit Corporation" as a legal corporate form. The goal is to create a business structure that rewards impact over profits.

Even this noble effort has its challenges. The certification process relies heavily on self-reported data and standardized scoring. This can incentivize "box-checking" rather than genuine transformation. While there are standards, they're not always consistently applied. B Corps are certainly a move in the right direction, but they don't necessarily solve the deeper problem: how do you truly measure whether lives are being changed or whether *your* mission is being accomplished?

The financial world is generally not built to see impact outcomes. It is built to view financial outcomes. Financial professionals are historically judged by balance sheets, not lives transformed. This misalignment stems from a lack of robust frameworks to measure impact as nonprofits do. If the financial world is going to continue to embrace impact investing, it will need a new approach, one that prioritizes purpose over profit.

LEARNING FROM NONPROFITS: THE LOGIC MODEL APPROACH

I hope it is becoming clear how the Purpose-Driven Capital Framework is designed to help the financial world consider purpose, at least in conjunction with profit. As you recall, logic models drive a mission to outcomes by thinking through inputs to activities to outputs to outcomes. This model demonstrates what it takes to create meaningful change to accomplish a mission. The outputs are measured, but they only matter when compared to the actual outcomes.

In the previous example, the amount of assistance provided was the output, but self-sufficiency was the ultimate outcome. And going back to our earlier example with the food distribution, the amount of food distributed was the output, but the number of families who were able to eventually move away from needing assistance was the real outcome.

A NEW APPROACH TO IMPACT METRICS

If you are seeking to engage in impact investing and you want to measure the actual impact your investment is having on a mission, I propose adopting a new mindset when thinking about how to measure it.

Returns are good: This is key! Some people feel guilty about accepting returns on their impact investing. Investing is not philanthropy. If the latter is your intent, then by all means, give. However, if you are investing, take the returns. Many investors do this in a philanthropic manner, but with an investor's mind. A term often used for this is regenerative philanthropy. They will reinvest their returns into the original project or another meaningful project to them.

Mission-focused outcomes: This goes back to starting with the end in mind. Once you know what you're aiming to achieve, determine the outcomes. Find a way to put a number on that. Then look at the outputs and determine the meaningful metrics that lead to those outcomes.

Ensure it's reported: This may seem a little ridiculous to include, but when it comes to impact investing, the outcomes are often left to be assumed. Frankly, this has been sufficient for a long time. It was true for nonprofits, too, until that sector grew and funding became highly competitive. As the impact investing landscape continues to grow in its adoption, reporting will need to scale as well as impact investing opportunities continue to institutionalize their impact demonstration.

GOOD SIGNS

You can tell that everything is going well when the expectations you set from the beginning are being met in the way you anticipated, based on your initial planning and reverse engineering of the process. Once you understand what you want to achieve, you'll be able to determine whether you're still on track or if things have diverged.

However, if things do go off track, it isn't necessarily a bad thing. It might be due to pursuing different goals—or even better ones. However, by monitoring, you have made yourself aware of the situation, and because you are aware, you can ask good questions.

It's valuable to seek clarity, either individually, with fellow investors or donors, or in a public context, by looking at the available information, as it empowers everyone. When everyone has awareness, it creates both accountability and opportunities to build on other people's thoughts.

PARTNERSHIP EXCLUSIONS SCREEN AND ACTIONS

In values-based investing, spending, or giving, maintaining an ongoing exclusions screen is highly valuable. People change, organizations evolve, and circumstances shift, so it's important to continually assess whether these exclusions are being violated by the capital actors involved. There are several ways to approach this.

When it comes to spending, you have less control over what happens after an expense is made. However, with donations or investments, there is a long-term relationship that must be nurtured. Over time, an organization may engage in activities that conflict with your exclusions, and it's up to you to stay informed about these changes.

In situations where you may be a significant contributor to the organization, you may be able to establish an Exclusions Commitment Progress Report. This report lists your Exclusions one-by-one, with checkboxes and a place for the company representative to sign. The idea is that you communicate to them that you appreciate what they do and that you plan to continue to support them as long as these Exclusions aren't violated.

At predetermined intervals, you can evaluate this list and confirm with the organization, in writing or another format, whether they are complying with those exclusions. A simple signature from them is sufficient for your records. You are keeping a record of accountability.

As the capital provider, it is your responsibility to ensure that these actors adhere to their commitments. Especially in long-term relationships, it is valuable to set expectations up front to avoid surprises later on, should questions arise about potential exclusions being violated.

If you discover that an organization has strayed from its commitments and is either violating an exclusion or failing to achieve expected outcomes, you have the three options from Chapter 7:

1. **Mitigation:** Can you take actions to minimize your involvement in any future harm caused by your capital?
2. **Redirection:** Is it possible to prevent the organization from future harm by eliminating the excluded activity entirely?
3. **Engagement:** Do you need to take a leadership role in addressing the issue internally?

If any of these actions can be pursued, you should attempt them. However, if you cannot take any of these steps, you may need to sever ties and seek reparations, not just for your losses but for the violations committed against your values.

By reparations, I'm simply referring to repairing any damage that your personal, direct involvement in that Capital Action may have caused. You may not have culpability, but there may be harm for which you have some responsibility. This is merely for consideration, as you will know the situation better than anybody.

FULFILL YOUR PURPOSE

While pursuing these actions may be extraordinary in its own right, it may also be virtuous to do so. The ultimate goal is to fulfill your purpose.

It's easy to feel overwhelmed by data, so keep things simple. Always ask yourself, *Is this capital actor progressing toward my mission? Are the outcomes aligned with my purpose? Are the means used to achieve these outcomes consistent with my Exclusions and the values they aspire to uphold?*

At the end of the day, ongoing assessment is not about numbers for their own sake. It is about ensuring clarity and accountability, so you can be confident and make decisions in line with your purpose. When you measure what truly matters and monitor it consistently, you protect your mission from drift and continue to guide your capital toward your intended outcomes. This way, you are giving structure to the responsibility you hold with the capital in your control. By keeping your outcomes aligned with your values, you turn good intentions into lasting impact, and you stay on the path to fulfilling your mission.

CHAPTER 9
BUILDING YOUR PURPOSE-DRIVEN CAPITAL SYSTEM

If our goal is to direct our capital toward genuine virtue in the pursuit of the good, the true, and the beautiful, we should systematize a process that simplifies our Capital Action decisions as an extension of who we are.

Now that you understand the process, it's time to build your system. You hold the power to intentionally drive the outcomes and fulfill your purpose.

Let's make it happen. This book provides a framework for you and your organization, uniquely designed to accomplish a particular purpose.

CASE STUDY: CENIARTH

There's a moment in every organization's life when the pieces no longer fit together, when what used to make sense suddenly feels like a contradiction. For Diane Isenberg, that moment came as she reviewed two very different sets of reports.

On one side were the grants Ceniarth had made: funding microfinance in rural communities, supporting smallholder farmers, and helping families build resilience at the edge of poverty. On the other side were the investment statements: traditional funds that were diversified and profitable but with no connection to those same communities.

She stared at the numbers and wondered, "Why are we separating the money we give from the money we invest?"

That question changed everything. Diane realized she wasn't just running a foundation with an endowment. She was stewarding a single pool of capital. Every dollar had the opportunity to either advance her mission or oppose it.

The first step was small. She directed a fraction of the portfolio into impact-first lending. This is capital that puts people, not profits, at the center. Would it work? Would the returns be enough? It was a test, but the results gave her confidence. Even in difficult markets, the capital did what it was meant to do. It served.

From there, the system began to take shape. Ceniarth organized its resources into three clear buckets:

1. Responsible assets for long-term security.
2. Programmatic funds blending grants and high-risk investments to catalyze innovation.
3. Impact-first capital where measurable change for people outweighed financial return.

By 2018, Ceniarth made a public commitment. Impact would come first, even when it meant trade-offs. Over time, grants, loans, and investments became inseparable parts of the same mission. A nonprofit that received a grant might later become the enterprise financed with a loan. An investment that preserves principal today could expand livelihoods tomorrow. Each piece of the puzzle reinforced the others.

Today, nearly half a billion dollars flows through this integrated platform. But the real takeaway for us is not about the amount of capital they are deploying. It's about the design of the system.

Ceniarth's story shows us something simple and powerful: The moment you stop separating your resources and start seeing them as one, clarity comes. That clarity is the beginning of your own framework.

You may not have hundreds of millions to deploy. But the same question still applies: How can every dollar I control serve my purpose? The answer is in the system you create. And now, it's your turn to design it.

BUILD YOUR SYSTEM

To some degree, we are all driven by the world's ways, and those ways either *pursue* us or *push* us to chase after ambition. But what does ambition really mean?

For some, ambition means becoming a billionaire. For others, it's simply about surviving and ensuring that their children reach a point of self-sufficiency.

So, what is ambition? What does it mean for each individual? This leads back to purpose, specifically, to your purpose-driven endeavors and the mission driving them.

What is your purpose? How are you working to fulfill it? I would argue that, for most people, their purpose doesn't tap into their full potential. We all have more capacity than what our current missions reflect.

We often overestimate what we can accomplish in a day while underestimating what we can achieve in a year. This idea resonates throughout our lives: We tend to overrate our daily accomplishments and, as a result, limit our aspirations, thinking we can only achieve so much in the short term. However, if we limit ourselves to what we can do today, we overlook our potential for remarkable achievements over an entire year.

We often fail to recognize the cumulative effect of our efforts as we progress. Therefore, I would argue that many people's missions aren't ambitious enough; we don't fully realize our potential and often become bogged down by the minutiae of daily life.

This is why we need a system to hold ourselves in check. That accountability will not only ensure that we are pursuing our mission but also that we aren't selling ourselves short. What COULD we accomplish if we really put our efforts in that direction? If we don't have a map, we likely aren't taking the straightest path toward our mission.

Your system should be tailored to reflect that purpose. This chapter will help you bring everything discussed in the book together to accomplish that goal. Remember, this is your chance to create a system that intentionally generates the outcomes you want to see in the world.

YOUR PURPOSE, PROCESS, AND OUTCOMES

The Purpose-Driven Capital Framework will streamline your decision-making process, ensuring alignment with your mission and goals. You will know your purpose because you have defined your mission: who you are, what you want to achieve, and how you plan to get there. You will understand your process, create assessments, and be guided through your purpose, Exclusions, and Elevations, which will lead you to your desired outcomes.

It will also shape your vision. How will you or your organization impact the world and leave a lasting legacy? Your system should become second nature.

The outcomes will naturally follow.

YOUR ADVERSARY THINKS YOU CAN'T DO IT

Your Adversary's final strategy is the most personal. They want you to believe that building a Purpose-Driven Capital system is too difficult, time-consuming, and idealistic, and is not worth the effort.

So, what does your Adversary want? They want you to admire the concept but doubt your ability to implement it. They want you to think that systematic purpose alignment is only for the super-wealthy, uber-organized, and ultra-disciplined.

You may be all or none of those, but your Adversary's strategy is to point to every complexity, every potential failure, every sacrifice required. They want the task to seem ridiculous. They want you to focus on all the reasons why it won't work rather than taking the first simple step.

So, what does your Adversary most fear you'll do? They fear that you'll start where you are. That you'll take your current resources and imperfectly start implementing your system with intention. They fear that you'll start seeing its compounding effort and how it continues to improve as you go.

Your Adversary has been building their systems for a long time. But here's what they don't expect. Once you begin aligning your capital with your purpose, the momentum builds quickly. Every aligned decision makes the next one easier. Every small victory builds confidence for bigger ones.

Ceniarth didn't become purpose-aligned overnight. They started with one decision, then another, then another.

Your Adversary is already at work. Your system is waiting to be built. The only question is: Will you start today?

YOUR PURPOSE. YOUR MISSION

Your purpose directs your mission. Ask yourself, *Why do I exist? What is my purpose? This purpose is my guiding direction, so how am I ensuring that I fulfill it?*

The first step is to know your Purpose Statement. Memorize it. Understand why you or your organization exists. Other important questions to consider are: Do others know what it is? Should they?

Remember, while your purpose is enduring, your mission is dynamic, not static. While it shouldn't change significantly, circumstances, people, and even you will evolve over time. These changes can lead to a refinement of your mission. Therefore, your mission statement is a living one. Does it reflect your current needs and the needs of the world today?

Does it capture your unique abilities to serve those needs? You should update it periodically, even revisiting it annually. While it should remain stable most of the time, be prepared for potential changes.

When you systematize Purpose-Driven Capital decisions, you create a feedback loop that keeps your Purpose Switch consistently activated. Each time you apply your mission assessment, Exclusions Screen, or Elevations priorities, you're reinforcing the neural pathways that connect financial choices with values alignment.

Over time, this systematic approach makes aligned decisions feel increasingly natural while misaligned decisions become noticeably uncomfortable. Your brain learns to associate your assessment process with the neurological reward of living according to your values. Eventually, the Purpose Switch activation becomes almost automatic—you'll find yourself instinctively applying your framework even in casual financial decisions because your brain has been trained to expect the satisfaction that comes from values-aligned choices.

YOUR PDC PROCESS

Your Purpose-Driven Capital process will ultimately lead to desired outcomes. If you recall the model, your Capital Actions influence your Capital Outcomes, all of which are driven by your Capital Impact Forces. These are defined by the lenses of Stewardship, Alignment, and Empowerment that you have created.

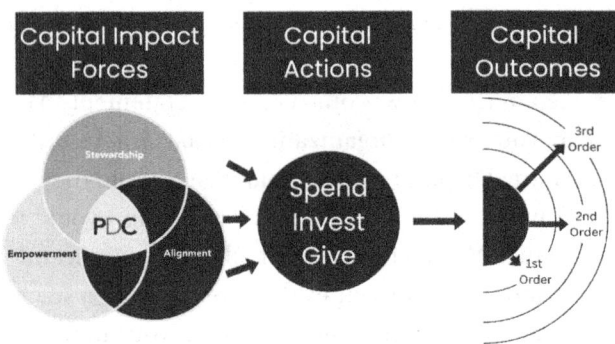

You determine how each of the Capital Impact Forces relates to your mission and how closely they collaborate to influence these Capital Actions. Initially, we focused on each force individually and how they impact each action. Now you can adopt a holistic view, where all the Capital Impact Forces work together to influence each action and determine the outcomes of those actions.

If you haven't developed your three Purpose-Driven Capital assessments yet, that should be your next step. Start by defining your purpose. Then create your three assessments, beginning with the purpose assessment. Keep it simple and create an Exclusions list.

Define your primary exclusions and assign weights to each one. You need to know how much weight each exclusion carries. Is it a non-negotiable aspect, or is it circumstantial? Clearly identify whether these

PURPOSE DRIVEN CAPITAL

exclusions are non-negotiable or circumstantial and assign the appropriate weight to each.

Next, create your Elevations list. Determine which key Elevations are most important to you and to what degree you want to pursue them. This is all about mindset. You should approach these three assessments as an extension of your mission in your daily life.

There's no need to memorize them; instead, revisit them regularly when making decisions. This process should become second nature over time.

EVALUATE YOUR OUTCOMES

As we discussed in the last chapter, be aware of your key metrics, your data sources, and the frequency of evaluation, and use your system to assess this data as it continues to yield outcomes over time.

Think about when you can find a regular time to assess your Capital Actions. Will it be daily, monthly, quarterly, annually, or every ten years? The more consistent it is, the simpler it will be to follow.

Make sure the appropriate people are present during these evaluations. If this is a personal mission, ensure that you are fully present. If this involves your team or organization, be sure to involve key stakeholders in the evaluation and decision-making process.

You can use this as a scorecard as you move forward. You have the time, the place, and the criteria for evaluation. This scorecard will help you assess whether you are progressing towards the outcomes you aimed for. From the insights gained, you can formulate an action plan. Then, at your next scheduled meeting, evaluate that action plan. Did you follow it? If so, what were the outcomes?

If you did not follow the plan, what adjustments are necessary? If the results were not what you hoped for, you can reassess the plan next year. The key is to have a structured system that guides you toward your goals, mission, and purpose.

IN WRITING, IN ONE PLACE

Document everything in one location. Keep a record of your entire system, including your evaluations and metrics. A three-ring binder can work, as can a folder on your computer. Ideally, maintain both a physical and a digital version for easy access. However, no matter which method you use, consistency is key.

This brings up two natural questions: Are you the only person who knows about this? Who else should be informed?

Consider whether leadership or other stakeholders are involved, such as coworkers or family members. If so, do they know where this information is documented? Is it easily accessible to them, allowing for ongoing evaluation with or without your involvement? You can find templates for all of this at purposedrivencapital.co.

Scan the QR code to access information templates:

CONCLUSION:
ONE SMALL STEP

Having reached his point, you may be thinking, *Where do I even start?* Perhaps you're worried that this is too much to take on and that you could never accomplish it all. I'm here to assure you that you definitely can, but like Diane Isenberg, it doesn't need to take place overnight.

Harkening back to Neil Armstrong's timeless quote, your "one small step" may have taken years of discernment and learning, but it can lead to generations of impact that otherwise could have never been achieved. What's more important is that you start.

PURPOSE-DRIVEN CHICKEN

By 2014, Chick-fil-A had become one of the most profitable fast-food chains per square foot in the country. They did so despite being open only 86 percent of the time compared to their competitors. However, they accomplished this not in spite of their system, but because of it. They weren't built on an ambition to be the biggest and most profitable restaurant chain. They were built on a purpose.

Before Chick-fil-A became a cultural icon, it was the vision of a man who saw business as a tool for a purpose. Its founder, Truett Cathy, wasn't just building a fast-food chain. He was building a system for faithful stewardship.

Cathy was a man of deep Christian conviction. To this day, the corporate Purpose Statement for the restaurant chain is "To glorify God by being a faithful steward of all that is entrusted to us. To have a positive influence on all who come in contact with Chick-fil-A."

Cathy believed that every business decision should be anchored in something greater than personal gain or quarterly profit. From the beginning, he made a bold and countercultural decision: Chick-fil-A would close every Sunday, no matter how much money it could make if it didn't.

For Cathy, this wasn't just about rest. It was about a clear call to his Christian faith. If God rested on the seventh day of creation, not only could Cathy do the same, but he should allow his people to rest as well. This became a non-negotiable exclusion for the company. He wanted his employees to have a day for faith, family, and restoration.

That decision has now become one of the most widely recognized purpose-driven exclusions in American business.

But the company's adherence to this mission went beyond Sunday closures. Cathy built a system that aligned people, capital, and purpose.

The hiring system is based on character, not just competency. Franchise ownership requires a unique commitment to culture, not just financial capital. Outcomes aren't solely measured by revenue but also by the positive influence on customers, team members, and communities.

The company even structures its corporate giving around youth development, education, and long-term community partnerships. Its mission serves as a compass and a map, with exclusions acting as guardrails that signal and embody its values. And the outcomes? They are measurable, generational, and legacy-shaping.

Now it's your turn.

THE PURPOSE-DRIVEN CAPITAL FRAMEWORK IS FOR YOU

You may be thinking that this sounds good, but it only applies to the super wealthy, people whose money can actually make big changes in the world.

In reality, what you're thinking about is influence. Regardless of how much money you have, you can create influence.

It doesn't even take money for you to have influence. By clicking on a website, you have influenced them by giving them your attention, which they then sell to make profits. Their entire business moves to best capture your clicks and attention. This can and has led to multi-billion-dollar pivots by massive tech and social media companies!

No matter where you are right now, this is not the time to hold back. This book is a road map, or shall I say, flight plan, for anyone.

I truly believe that each of us, as individuals and entities, was created with purpose, for a purpose. I believe that each of us has a duty to find a path to achieve that purpose. There is a path for you to do that and to drive it through your finances.

Let's get started!

YOUR STARTING POINT

You don't need to wait. You don't need a formal plan, nor do you have to assess various templates. You can begin right here and now, starting with your purpose.

Think about what you stand for. You likely have a greater purpose in your life or within your organization. What is that purpose?

PURPOSE STATEMENT

Do you already have a Purpose Statement? If so, great! If not, why not? Start brainstorming. Work through your ideas and see if you can brainstorm a working Purpose Statement today.

If you do have a Purpose Statement, does it accurately reflect your beliefs and the essence of your organization? Identify what needs refinement to ensure that it truly defines you or your organization. Clarifying your purpose is crucial.

ONE KEY OUTCOME

Next, identify one key outcome. What is one specific thing you want to achieve as a result of your financial decisions? Perhaps you aspire to establish a global organization with a meaningful goal. What is that one goal?

Alternatively, you might decide to do something simpler, more immediate. You want to ensure that farmers are treated well in the production of your coffee. So you commit to buying fair-trade certified coffee.

What is the one outcome you want to pursue today? While you may not accomplish it right away, you can begin the pursuit today. Focus on that one key outcome that matters so much to you that it takes priority over everything else.

PURPOSE IN MIND

Thirdly, start walking your path with purpose. Now that you know your mission, live it out immediately. You might not have all the details figured out yet, but you understand your purpose and why you exist. Start living that purpose every moment of every day because you are mindful of it. You'll be surprised at the changes you make.

Personally, I've experienced this, and countless others have, too. Once they start recognizing their purpose daily, they change their habits and behaviors. They catch themselves doing things they would normally do, but that contradict their purpose. Because they know their purpose, they consciously break those habits and choose more virtuous alternatives.

YOUR LEGACY

Finally, think about your long-term destination. Are you aiming for that billion-dollar foundation, or is your goal more family-oriented or relational? What is the long-term outcome you envision? Whether it's related to your key outcome or a broader destination for yourself, your family, or your organization, define that one destination you want to strive for. It is valuable to have the end in mind!

KEEP GROWING, KEEP ITERATING

Continuously develop your system. Regardless of whether you're just starting to draft your Purpose Statement or if you have a comprehensive system already in place, continue to build upon it. Identify the next piece or layer of depth that you need to add. Determine what steps you need to take to reach that ultimate destination.

Your system can help you reach your goals. Once you get there, whether it's today or further down the road, you should continue to develop your impact measurements. Refine them and figure out what those metrics mean. Consider how you can gain more meaningful insights from less data over time.

TRY IT: YOUR NEXT CAPITAL ACTION

Next, think about your Capital Actions through this new lens. After defining your purpose and understanding the key outcome you're pursuing, you're beginning to follow that path. With a long-term destination in mind and your system in motion, consider the measurements you've established. What Capital Action can you take next, and how can you approach it with a mission-driven, purpose-driven perspective?

YOUR ADVERSARY IS ALREADY AT WORK AGAINST YOU

The reality is that your Adversary is already taking action. No matter how long it takes you to implement your strategy, they are seizing every moment you leave unfilled. They're placing their systems and taking advantage of opportunities that arise as you focus elsewhere. If you fail to act today, your Adversary will gain the upper hand.

Your Adversary will dominate whatever aspects you don't want to see them control unless you make the conscious decision to counteract them. Consider the people mentioned in this book like Tim Tebow and Tom Monaghan. They have navigated their lives with a Purpose-Driven Capital focus, despite following unique paths and very different headwinds.

YOUR CAPITAL, YOUR MISSION

Anyone who is spending, investing, or giving any amount of money can apply the Purpose-Driven Capital Framework to create a world of virtue and pursue the good, the true, and the beautiful.

In my Christian tradition, there is a story of a woman who gave two mites, or small copper coins. Although a small amount of money, Jesus says that she gave more than anybody else because it was all that she had. The story may not illustrate a huge change in the world due to her financial giving, but her example, immortalized by the Gospels, has been used to teach Christians about eternity.

In the same way, we may never know the total impact of our actions. So, it is imperative that we think of every reaction, especially actions with our money, as having infinite value, because they demonstrate where our hearts are and what we want to see more of in the world.

Truett Cathy didn't build Chick-fil-A around a business plan or a mission statement. He built it around a Purpose Statement—a single line that has guided every decision long after he was gone. That's Purpose Driven Capital in action.

This is your capital, and this is your purpose. You can start today. There's no need to overcomplicate matters; just take the initiative with one small step. Use the Purpose-Driven Capital Framework to progressively build your system to align your resources with your mission.

Understand your purpose, define your mission, and outline your process. Identify each of those impact forces, ensure your three assessments are in place, and guide your desired outcomes based on these assessments to accomplish your mission and fulfill your purpose.

The best time to start was with your first dollar. The second-best time is today. You can do this, so get started now!

ACKNOWLEDGMENTS

First and always, to God, the Author of Life, and Giver of every good thing, and through Christ His Son, hope for eternal salvation for a sinner like me.

To Mal, Lucy, and Blaise. You are my favorite people. I treasure every moment with you. I could not ask for a better support system or people to spend life with.

To my parents. I will never fully know how much you sacrificed for me. You offered a loving home with every opportunity a kid could want or need. Even today, you still continue to support me. I can never thank you enough for all you still do for me and, now, more importantly, for my family.

To my sister, who, in spite of countless hours of drum practice on the other side of the wall from my room and my merciless jokes, is still the greatest of supporters. Your love and loyalty are an undeserved gift. I can only hope that a fraction of the grace and love you give to others has rubbed off on me. And Joe, thank you for loving Christy and our whole family. Your joy and insight uplift us all!

To my wife's family. From the beginning, you welcomed me into the family as if it had always been that way. Mal and I are so grateful for all you do with and for us!

To Bobby. You planted the seed for this book. You are a gift from God to all those around you!

To Fr. Bart. Your patient guidance threaded a difficult needle, being both pastor and boss. You helped me professionally and drew me deeper into faith and reason... lifelong lessons that continue to shape me.

To my colleagues, board members, volunteers, and, of course, donors at Catholic Charities. You all taught me about intentional sacrifice for others and loving them for their inherent dignity.

To Tom Monaghan. You unwittingly inspired a LOT of this book. When we first met, I was surprised that you were exactly the person that I had read about, joyful and relentlessly focused on your mission. God is clearly working in you and through you.

To Felipe Witchger and the Francesco Collaborative. Thank you for welcoming me and challenging my thinking. You introduced me to a side of impact investing I had never known.

To Dan Schreck and all who attended the Ave Maria University Investing for Good Symposium. I realized there that I was not alone in thinking that there is more to impact investing and provided a deep intellectual perspective that is neglected in the mainstream.

To my coach, Brian. Whether it was big ideas, moments of success, imposter syndrome, feeling directionless, or just having a bad week, you helped me refocus and redirected me toward my purpose.

To my podcast guests. I love our conversations! Thank you for your time and insights with me. Special shout-out to Marla Sofer. Your discussion on nonprofits ignited a lot of the thinking behind this book.

To the entire Game Changer Publishing team. I am so grateful for your guidance, creativity, and encouragement. And Taygen, I am forever grateful for your patient ears and guided questions.

Finally, to all who offered support in my times of need and grace when I did not deserve it. Thank you for the impact you have had on me.

THANK YOU FOR READING MY BOOK!

Download Your Free Gifts
Just to say thanks for buying and reading my book, I would like to give you a few free bonus gifts, no strings attached!

To Download Now, Visit:

I appreciate your interest in my book and value your feedback, as it helps me improve future versions of this book. I would appreciate it if you could leave your invaluable review on Amazon.com with your feedback.
Thank you!

NOTES

INTRODUCTION

1. The 2025 Wells Fargo Money Study. Accessed September 22, 2025. https://sites.wf.com/wfmoneystudy-2025/media/Money-Study-Full-Report-2025.pdf.

1. FUND YOUR PURPOSE, DEFEAT YOUR ADVERSARY

1. Address at Rice University on the nation's space effort, September 12, 1962 | JFK library. Accessed September 22, 2025. https://www.jfklibrary.org/archives/other-resources/john-f-kennedy-speeches/rice-university-19620912.

3. YOUR PURPOSE. YOUR MISSION

1. Misaligned values in software engineering organizations. Accessed September 22, 2025. https://www.researchgate.net/publication/329399018_Misaligned_values_in_software_engineering_organizations.

4. PURPOSE ALIGNMENT AND THE CAPITAL IMPACT FORCES

1. People Possibility. "The Power of Alignment in the Workplace: Why It Matters and How to Achieve It." People Possibility, November 11, 2024. https://peoplepossibility.com/the-power-of-alignment-in-the-workplace-why-it-matters-and-how-to-achieve-it/?utm.

6. ELEVATIONS: OPPORTUNITIES TO ADVANCE YOUR MISSION

1. The terms "blue ocean" and "red ocean" were originally introduced in the book *Blue Ocean Strategy* by W. Chan Kim and Renee Mauborgne (Harvard Business Review Press, 2005).

7. DECISION, DILIGENCE, AND DISCERNMENT

1. "What You Need to Know about Impact Investing." The GIIN. Accessed November 13, 2025. https://thegiin.org/publication/post/about-impact-investing/#what-is-impact-investing.

Disclaimer

This book is solely for educational purposes and should not be relied on as investment advice. The author has produced this book independently from any broker-dealer or investment advisory firm with which the author may be associated. No securities regulatory authority has approved the information contained in this book.